why fear?

JOHN DEVRIES

why fear?

Forty-Two Reasons not to be Afraid,
from Psalm 23

Grand Rapids, Michigan

WHY FEAR? © 2013 by John DeVries

Published by
Project Philip Ministries
Grand Rapids, MI 49512

www.projectphilipministries.org

ISBN: 978-0-9884202-2-9

Design by Michael Lautenbach

First Printing, 2013

*For my group at Plymouth who, without knowing it, played a
great role in the development of this book.
Their enthusiasm continues to inspire.*

*And to my wife Adelaide, with whom I have prayed
each morning for so many years and from whom I have learned
these lessons in freedom from fear.*

*And in grateful thanks and recognition to Darlene Morrow
whose tireless efforts in editing and grammar have*

been a tremendous gift of God!

Dr. John DeVries is the founder of two Christian nonprofit organizations; Project Philip and Mission India. For over forty years John has worked and prayed diligently to equip God's people to be "Philips" in both the United States and in India. John invites you to visit the Project Philip Ministries website at www.projectphilipministries.org or the Mission India website at www.missionindia.org.

4180 44th SE Suite A

Grand Rapids, MI 49512-4057

contents

introduction

At one time or another, everyone has had some reason to feel afraid: rejection, sickness, war, poverty, loss, death—you name it. There are many circumstances that can trigger this emotion. This little book shows you how to banish fear and enjoy peace by studying Psalm 23, the most well-known Psalm in the Bible.

John DeVries picks seven reasons "not to be afraid" from each of the six verses. As you apply these reasons to the fears that particularly trouble you, God can give you a new freedom from fear, and with that freedom, a new peace: "And the peace of God, which transcends all understanding, will guard your hearts and your minds in Christ Jesus" (Philippians 4:7).

We must remember what Jesus said in John 14:27: "Peace I leave with you; my peace I give you. I do not give to you as the world gives. Do not let your hearts be troubled … and do not be afraid."

We will be studying each of the six verses in Psalm 23 as a separate section with six sections in all. If you wish to use this book as a daily devotional, read one devotional a day. Each of the six sections is divided into seven thoughts for seven days. In each section we will examine seven words or phrases from each verse in more devotional depth. Begin each meditation by slowly repeating Psalm 23 in its entirety. If you "take" Psalm 23 daily for 42 days, it will drive most fears away. Below are the general themes of each section.

Section One—*Belonging:* Each verse in this beautiful little poem contains many ways in which we can overcome our fears. The first verse deals with the concept of belonging. We all need to belong. Belonging is the deepest emotional and spiritual need a human has. Loneliness causes fear. Belonging banishes both loneliness and the fear resulting from being alone. We were created in God's image, which means we were created to belong to him and to each other in love. True love is the cement that bonds us together. Loving Jesus as our shepherd sets us free from loneliness and fear.

Section Two—*Provision:* We need peace, and verse 2 shows how a shepherd provides peace for his sheep by leading them to secure places, making certain they are free from fear, friction, flies, and famine. Jesus gives the peace that is beyond the power of positive thinking or the manipulation of the mind. As we experience all the meaning included in "green pastures and quiet waters," we will experience some of that mysterious peace. We will discover new ways to overcome our fears.

Section Three—*Restoration:* In verse 3 David talks about restoration to wholeness. In Ephesians 1, Paul speaks to this in terms of a "mystery of God's will." Even though all the king's horses and all the king's men could not put Humpty Dumpty together again, Jesus is able to put us back together again. Our shepherd, Jesus, brings us back together in love. God is putting everything in the universe back together again. Upon restoration to a right relationship with God through Jesus Christ, we enter the supernatural world of freedom from fear.

Section Four—*Protection:* Verse 4 speaks about ultimate protection. We will all walk through the valley of the shadow of death. Jesus is there to guard us. We don't like to think about death, but it is certain that we will one day die bodily. No one except Jesus has gone through death's point of no return and returned to tell about it. He shepherds us through this mystery of death.

Section Five—*Victory:* To follow Jesus means that his power flows into us, and his authority crowns us. Christians in India understand power, especially over demons and their demonic strongholds. The excitement and wonder of repeated victories over demonic power drives the spontaneous growth of the Indian church in perhaps the greatest spread of the gospel in history.

Section Six—Security: Verse 6 ends with security, both in this life and forever. We will dwell in

God's house forever, after a life filled with goodness and mercy. Here are the real, everlasting
reasons for celebration. They are the blessings of
eternal life, which we can begin to enjoy now, in
time.

FLOAT IT!

"Float it!" Float what? Float the verses of Psalm 23 in your mind. Do so with a verse a week. As you read the meditations on each verse, start each day by "floating" that verse in your mind. Repeat it a few times before you even get out of bed. Keep repeating it throughout the day, and throughout the week. When you face a decision, or when a fear creeps in, recite the verse. Look at everything through the spiritual lens of this verse and you will be surprised at what will happen to you.

As I wrote this book, I did this with my group at church. I had them "float" the verse I was working on and then as we got together, we shared what Jesus was telling us in that verse. We did it for each of the six verses of Psalm 23. It was a profound, moving, joy-filled experience, and through it, our little group changed. We spent our times together talking about answered prayer, and our excitement and joy increased as we saw the amazing, unexpected answers to our prayers unfold.

We discovered together that prayer is more than a one-way, oft times boring, monologue in which we do all the talking, and Jesus does the listening. Jesus talks to us through the words of the Bible, for the words of Scripture have been inspired by his Holy Spirit. As we memorized a verse a week, taking it with us throughout the day, we discovered that Jesus was talking to us through the verse. We were learning to be quiet and to listen. As we listened to his guidance in the verse, we not only found that our fears were beginning to fade, we also found amazing solutions to the "little" things that irritate us so much. Together we experienced the comfort of being guided each day by The Shepherd, Jesus.

Floating a verse in your mind each day and then sharing your experiences with your family or group will be a transforming experience! Don't just read this book—experience it in love with others.

-John DeVries

Belonging

The Lord is my shepherd, I shall not want

— Psalm 23:1

Each verse in this beautiful little poem contains many ways in which we can overcome our fears. The first verse deals with the concept of belonging. We all need to belong. Belonging is the deepest emotional and spiritual need a human has. Loneliness causes fear. Belonging banishes both loneliness and the fear that results from being alone. We were created in God's image, which means we were created to belong to him and to each other, in love. True love is the cement that bonds us together. Loving Jesus as our shepherd sets us free from loneliness and fear.

DAY 1

Float this verse and highlighted word in
your mind throughout the day.

The Lord is my shepherd,
I shall not want.

— Psalm 23:1

Here is how we will work—we will take seven words
or phrases from a verse, one per reading, and see
what happens to our fear when we understand the
rich meaning each holds. Each word will be in bold
print. So of course, the first word is "the." Now don't
laugh, and don't close the book. You just might be
surprised at what marvelous thoughts about freedom from fear can be found in that little word, "the."

Many years ago I was standing in line in the college commons waiting to pay for my coffee when
she came down the opposite line and flashed
her amazing smile at me. Suddenly the word *the*

popped into my head as I thought, "Hey, that's *the* one for me."

Apparently the message hadn't gotten to her quite yet. She turned me down for a date four times. I assured her that my fifth invitation was the last, and she relented. That was the beginning. Four years later we were married, and for these 54 years since, she has been *the* one for me. Do you see how important that little word "*the*" is in that context?

The definite article *the* sets things and people apart. It can put people on a pedestal, too. For instance, the "One" who takes away our fear is not just a lord; Jesus is *the* LORD. This is why he could frequently tell his disciple not to be afraid: "Peace I leave with you; my peace I give you. I do not give to you as the world gives. Do not let your hearts be troubled, and do not be afraid" (John 14:27). Jesus is *the* source: the only source, the greatest source of freedom from fear. He is exceptional. He is the one who can stop us from being afraid.

We use *the* when we describe something exceptional. We describe an exceptional person as "the" person, or a vacation as "the" vacation of a lifetime. Think of falling in love. "I've found the one," our teenager declares upon falling in love for the first time.

Everyone longs to belong. God made us in his image, and that means we were created to belong to him and to each other. We are his relatives—his children. There are many levels of belonging, all of which combined make up our identity. We belong to our family. We belong to clubs. We belong to a circle of friends. We belong to the place where we live. We belong to schools and other institutions. Security comes from belonging. Fear comes from insecurity.

Around 1550, during the turbulence of the Protestant Reformation in Europe, when many people were being thrown in jail and even burned at the stake for their belief in Jesus, two young men wrote the following words and threw them over the emperor's palace wall as a testimony of *the* person to whom they belonged. It began with the question, "What is your only comfort in life and in death?" Here is their answer.

My only comfort is…
That I am not my own,
But belong –
In body and soul
In life and in death –
To my faithful Savior Jesus Christ.
He has fully paid for all my sins with his precious
blood,
And has set me free from the tyranny of the devil.
He also watches over me in such a way
That not a hair can fall from my head
Without the will of my Father in heaven;
In fact, all things must work together for my
salvation.
Because I belong to him,
Christ by his Holy Spirit,
Assures me of eternal lifeAnd makes me
wholeheartedly willing and ready
From now on to live for Him.

— *Heidelberg Catechism Q @ A 1*

The one and only source of freedom from fear is belonging to Jesus. He is *the* shepherd. He is *the* ultimate One. He is *the* beginning and *the* end. And when he calls you, and you hear his voice, an eternal bond is created, and you belong to him for eternity. As Norman Clayton wrote in his famous hymn:

> *Now I belong to Jesus*
>
> *Jesus belongs to me*
>
> *Not for the years of time alone*
>
> *But for eternity.*

In the midst of the business of your life, your successes and your failures, celebrate *the* today. Thank God that you have found *the* source of protection, direction, and provision. Our shepherd, Jesus, stands above the crowd as the LORD, the only source of freedom from fear.

Reflect:
No other god can do today what Jesus, our shepherd, can do. Recall how you came to belong to him. Is he the one for you? Why is belonging to Jesus the ultimate place to belong, and how does belonging to him quiet and remove your fears?

DAY 2

Float this verse and highlighted word in
your mind throughout the day.

The **Lord** is my shepherd, I
shall not want.

—Psalm 23:1

I was born twenty-five pounds overweight, a condition from which I have yet to recover. Obviously the first part of that sentence is not true. As to the second part, I'll leave it up to those who know me. Suffice it to say, my friends and family have been known to call me "Fat Stuff," a term of affection that has had reason to stick for a long time.

Nevertheless, being called "Fat Stuff" didn't do much for my self-image. What we think of ourselves, how we look at ourselves, and what we identify with and belong to…all are ingredients of our self-image. We can become afraid when we don't look "good", or when we don't belong, or when we are failures. But ironically, even when we are successful, we can be afraid that we will fail; when we are rich, we can fear that we will lose all and become poor. Even if we are powerful, as is the President of the United States, we can fear that we won't be re-elected or that our critics will pull us down.

Fred Lybrand, in *Heavenly Citizenship*, puts it this way: "Identity can be determined from thousands of sources. I'm married. I'm single. I'm a parent. I belong to this city. I'm a Texan. I'm an American, proud to be an American. I do this job. Or on the negative side, perhaps I don't have this job. I'm white. I'm black. I'm Hispanic . . ." (p.7). We identify ourselves by associating ourselves with different people, things, and work.

At the middle school graduation of one of our children I used four balloons to represent the four major factors on which we often base our value, worth, and identity. We use our possessions, repu-tation, looks, and deeds to determine our worth. These four factors are about as fragile as four balloons. How much do I own? What do people say about me, and what important people are my friends? Am I handsome or homely? What have I accomplished? The answers to these questions shape our self-image. Those who seek their identity in these temporal things will always live in fear because every one of the earthly things by which we identify ourselves is like a balloon that pops with the slightest pin prick.

I popped each balloon with a nice loud bang to illustrate the jolts of life. I'm not rich...*pop* goes the balloon of wealth. I'm not handsome or cute...*pop* goes the balloon of looks. I'm not liked...*pop* goes the balloon of reputation. I'm a failure...*pop* goes the balloon of success. The things in which we find our identity are so fragile! As long as we build our identity on the passing things of this earth, we will be as fragile as a balloon, and emotionally, we will be like a broken balloon.

From these first two words of Psalm 23, *the Lord*, we discover the ultimate solution to attain freedom from fear. It is an eternal, unshakable identity firmly rooted in belonging to the LORD, who is the creator and ruler of the universe.

While floating down the Colorado River I was impressed with the huge boulders lining the river banks. Great chunks of the rock walls had cracked off and fallen down. I had to laugh as I thought of lifting one of them. I compared the little rock I could lift with these massive boulders. I thought of Jesus, the one who could not only lift them, but who also created them. I laughed again as I thought of his incredible strength, compared to my weakness. I thought of his timelessness, compared to my short life. And in my mind's eye I curled up in the comfort of knowing that the LORD is my shelter. He is the reason I do not have to fear.

We are made in his image and likeness. Jesus is the Creator of the universe. "Through him all things were made; without him nothing was made that has been made" (John 1:3). We are "the glory of God" because we reflect him. We live and move only because he gives us air to breathe and he sustains our bodies, souls and spirits. We belong to him. When we understand and trust that we belong to Jesus, we will experience amazing freedom from fear. We will feel and be so close to him that we can call him our shepherd.

Look around you at the sky, at the stars, at the fish, at the birds, at the flowers, and at the trees. The God who made this all, the LORD of the universe, is our provider, protector, and director. This LORD is our shepherd. He is eternal. He is infinite love. He does not change. You cannot destroy him with a pin prick, or with a bomb.

There is a little song that sums it up well: "I'm a child of the King, a child of the King, with Jesus my Savior I'm a child of the King." Jesus said that unless we become as carefree little children in the way in which we fully trust him, we cannot get into the kingdom of heaven (Matthew 18:3).

Take the word LORD with you today. Banish your fears with the thought that it is the LORD who is your shepherd, your Savior, your source of strength, the answer to all your prayers, your guide in all of life's problems and challenges, and the One who owns you forever. Relax in belonging to Jesus, in being loved by the LORD of the universe. Let the joy of belonging to the LORD forever fill your day. Roll the idea over and over in your mind. You are secure forever

Reflect:
In what ways do you build your identity? How do these ways add to your fears? What is your reaction to building your identity on belonging to Jesus, the LORD of all?

DAY 3

The Lord **is** my shepherd; I shall not want.

—Psalm 23:1

What does "*is*" mean? Isn't it interesting how the littlest of words can be so significant? What is the meaning of such a tiny, constantly-used word? It denotes the third-person, singular form of the verb form *to be* (i.e., existence); but perhaps most significantly, its tense is the present. It refers to the now, to the reality in which we live at a moment. For instance, "is" something for real or "is" it only a dream? And more to the point in our passage here: Is Jesus' being my shepherd merely something I have read and known only intellectually, or "is" Jesus being my shepherd a constant, daily, immediate experience?

Ask a college student if she knows the material for a test, and she says, "Yes," because she has studied hard to prepare. But ask her if she believes it, and she might respond, "Does that matter?" All she needs to *know* is the material; she doesn't have to *believe* it in order to pass the course.

To say "Jesus *is* my shepherd" means that you both know the fact and that you also believe in it. And believing in it makes a profound difference in conquering fear. Is Jesus' shepherding so real that you are aware of it at every moment and enjoy the comfort that it brings constantly?

One of the greatest temptations that we constantly face is to do a good that Jesus hasn't called us to do. We substitute the good we want to do for the good God calls us to do. We burn ourselves out, becoming afraid and depressed. We are often both blind and deaf to the leading of Jesus. We want to go our own way, and it may be a good way; but it's often not the one upon which Jesus is guiding us.

When we substitute the good we want to do for going where our shepherd is leading, fear sets in. We become confused. We become discouraged. We think we know better than Jesus, and the little word *is* disappears. He no longer "is" our guide. We are not allowing Jesus to be our shepherd when we select the good we want to do and walk the path we choose rather than the path he selects. Wandering sheep always become afraid.

To say that Jesus "is" our shepherd means that we end each day celebrating how Jesus led us in the tiny and the large things of that day. More often, however, we have been too busy doing our own thing to have listened for the leading God is giving. We plan and then we ask God to bless our plans, but God already has his own blessed plans for us. Why would God bless our plans, when he has better plans for us?

Our prayer should always be, "Show me, Jesus, my shepherd, what your plans for me are today. Where are you guiding me? What do you want me to do?" We must stop putting our will first, even if we believe it is for the good, because so often it may keep us from doing the good that Jesus wants us to do. Often our prayers are pleading for Jesus to do what we want, rather than asking him to show us what he wants us to do. This always results in fear.

To say that Jesus "is" my shepherd means that

I am continuously listening to his prompting for direction. Asking for Jesus to show us his will and then to enable us to do it is the way to conquer fear.

We need to share encouraging stories of how the LORD leads us out of fear and depression. We need more than the knowledge that Jesus is the ultimate solution for fear. We need the experience that this truth "is" true in our lives.

I once had a horrendous assignment to lead all-day seminars in several cities on a daily basis. After doing one seminar I would travel at night to the next city. I would lead the seminar there, and then in the late afternoon I would head for the airport to fly to the next city. I did these seminars four or five times a week for four weeks. When it was over, I returned home in total exhaustion. I lay on the sofa, stared at the ceiling, and said nothing.

Toward eleven o'clock that night my wife knelt beside me. I knew she was praying when suddenly I sat up and looked at her. "What are you doing? What is going on?" The black depression had suddenly lifted.

She laughed. "Oh great King Tut [she has a

unique sense of humor], I told the demons to leave you alone in the name of Jesus Christ. It appears they left."

It was an "is" moment in my life that I have never forgotten. Christ stepped in and set me free from the fear that I deserved for the crazy way I had been working. Even though I had been "working for the LORD," I had not listened to him, and in weariness, I sunk into depressing fear. In an awesome, powerfully-freeing way, Christ answered my wife's prayer and sent me a peace, joy, and quietness that transformed me instantly.

Each of us will have our own, unique moments when we will experience the wonder of the truth that Jesus "is" our shepherd. These epiphanies will be experiences to which we return often in battling new doubts and depressions.

Have you moved beyond "knowing" that Jesus is the ultimate source of freedom from fear to a few wonderful experiences of living in it?

Reflect:
Recall moments of fear when Jesus came and set you free.

DAY 4

The Lord is **my** shepherd, I
shall not want.

— Psalm 23:1

In a book of meditations called, Who Do You Look
Like?, I tell the story of another discovery in my life.
Because of the nickname, "Fat stuff," I struggled
with my identity, suffering periodic depression
accompanied by continuous anxiety. While I knew
Christ as Savior, I struggled with the word my. What
did it mean to call Jesus "my" shepherd? It always
seemed to me that he was like a shepherd, outside
of me, watching over me, carrying me. There had to
be more to the relationship than that, more to the
meaning of my.

"Footprints in the Sand" is a well-known little
story in which a person imagines walking with
Jesus, and seeing two sets of footprints, side-
by-side in the beach sand. But suddenly trouble

strikes, and difficulties come. And at that moment, just one set of footprints can be seen. Christ's companion looks at the single set of footprints and is perplexed. "Where did you go during my trouble?" she asks. Jesus replies, "When you saw only one set of footprints, it was then that I carried you." I have felt that there must be more than merely having Jesus carry me in times of trouble, however. Isn't our bond, our reason to call Jesus "my" shepherd, deeper than that? I thought of the words of that wonderful old spiritual: "Were you there when they crucified my Lord? O, sometimes it causes me to tremble—tremble. Were you there when they crucified my Lord?"

I couldn't figure that song out. How could I have been there? Of course I was not there. Or was I? What does it mean to be "in" Christ? Is that related to calling Jesus "my" shepherd? Imagine three tennis balls in a can. If I bury the can, the balls are also buried. If I dig the can up, the balls are also dug up. What happens to the can also happens to the tennis balls in the can. When Jesus died on the cross and suffered the consequences of sin, my being spiritually "in him" means that I, with all my sins, have suffered the punishment with him. So Christ is now also "my" eternal protection against all punishment for sin. I am in him and thus cleansed by his sacrifice for me. What happens to the can also happens to the tennis balls. What happened to Jesus, also happened to me, because of the word *my*. I am "in" him. He is *my* source of freedom, *my* protector, and *my* provider. He doesn't merely carry me; I am in him like tennis balls are in a can. I am in his kingdom, in his family; I am among his possessions.

Likewise, there are two sides in the war of the universe: There is Satan's side, and there is Christ's side. Are you "in" Christ's realm or in that of the evil one? Christ's side is the victorious side. Can you say, "That's *my* side"? If I am on Christ's side, then I am with him spiritually now, as he sits in glory. I don't have to be afraid, for he has won the victory. *And God raised us up with Christ and seated us with him in the heavenly realms in Christ Jesus* (Eph. 2:6).

Jesus told us that he is the vine and we are the branches (John 15:1-5). Just as branches are in the vine so we are *in* Christ. We are together. I am where my shepherd is, for I am in him, in his flock, on his side. I was in his arms when he suffered eternal punishment on Calvary, and I am also in his arms now as he rules the world. Just think—I can say he is my shepherd, because I have been, and am now, spiritually in his arms. Now that is freedom from fear!

There is more, however. God tells us in the Bible that Jesus is also in us. It isn't just that we are in Jesus; he, through his Holy Spirit, is now in us. To call Jesus my shepherd doesn't stop with being *in him*. He is *in us*: *I have been crucified with Christ and I no longer live, but Christ lives in me* (Gal. 2:20).

I'm looking at a lamp on my desk right now. It has four parts: a base, a socket in which I screw the bulb, a chord to plug into a power source, and a switch to turn it on and off. Jesus said that he is the light of the world, but he also claimed that we are the light of the world. How can both be true at the same time? The answer is simple: When Jesus is my shepherd, his light shines through me. I am the lamp and shade, and he is the "bulb." The chord is the Holy Spirit's power flowing into me. The switch is my faith and awareness that Christ, the light of the world, is in me and wants to shine out of me.

When I am aware of that, and believe that, and celebrate that, I turn on the switch so that Christ, the light of the world, shines out of me. The peace and courage radiating from my face is a sign that Jesus has banished my fears. As I pray for persons and areas, I focus the spotlight of Christ's light on those persons and areas.

Reflect:
How does your relationship with Christ as being both in him and he being in you, set you free from fear and fill you with joy?

DAY 5

The Lord is my **shepherd**,
I shall not want.

—Psalm 23:1

I'm thankful that God is not a "cowboy." No offense to cowboys, but just think about it. Cowboys are not exactly known for their gentle touch when it comes to handling their livestock.

Come branding time, how is a calf treated by a cowboy? Torn from its mother, it runs panic-stricken in front of a man on a horse who swirls a long rope, lands it on its neck, and jerks it to a painful halt. Dismounting, the cowboy runs up to the calf, grabs its head, and twists it, throwing it to the ground. His legs are then tied up, and the calf lays, helpless and terror-stricken, bawling.

As if that weren't bad enough, a red hot branding iron is quickly pressed onto its hind quarter, filling the air with the stench of its burning hair.

Finally, the panic-stricken creature is released to gallop away to its mother. (Wouldn't you?) I'm so thankful that God's method of operating is not that of the cowboy.

Instead, God presents himself as a shepherd. Through the eyes of King David (whose former occupation was shepherd) we see the LORD as a shepherd—David's shepherd and ours—the one who owns the sheep. Jesus accepted this title when he said: "I am the good shepherd. The good shepherd lays down his life for the sheep" (John 10:11). His sheep know him, and he knows his sheep. The shepherd and his sheep belong to each other. This means that if Jesus is our shepherd, the king and creator of the universe protects us to the point of laying down his own life for us. That is precisely what Jesus has done. Thus, when we are his sheep (or in other words, when we belong to Jesus), we have no reason to fear. He will care for us, and because he lives, all fear is gone.

Sheep belong to the shepherd. Jesus said: "I am the good shepherd; I know my sheep and my sheep know me" (John 10:14). Belonging to Jesus is not merely an abstract idea; he knows us, and we know him. This means that we belong to him in the deepest and richest sense of the word, and this belonging is the greatest cure for fear there is.

When I am afraid, I love to sing a few lines from a little hymn by Norman Clayton: "Now I belong to Jesus, / Jesus belongs to me, / Not for the years of time alone, / But for eternity." Belonging to Jesus involves eternal protection, but far more than that—it includes having an everlasting love relationship with the God of creation.

A shepherd does not drive his sheep to slaughter, but plans each day with great care. He leads them to the finest pastures and to quiet waters. And when a little lamb is lost, he leaves everything to find it; when he does find it, he gently carries it in his arms back to safety. Jesus said that a good shepherd will even die for his sheep. Yes, I am so glad God is a shepherd. Shepherds know their sheep, and their sheep know them.

We don't know how old David was when he wrote this little Psalm, but there is reason to believe that he wrote it near the end of his life. He looked back through the turmoil and bloodshed of the wars. He looked beyond being chased by Saul. He looked back to those peaceful teenage years when he wandered the hills with his father's sheep, seeking food, water, and rest for them. He remembered those frightful moments of protecting them from the wild animals and how those sheep were free of fear, because he was with them. He thought of how they knew his voice and responded to his call. And he pictured himself as a little lamb in the arms of the infinite shepherd, and his peace was restored again. He recalled times of victory and, times of disgrace and failure; times of trust and times when his faith waned; times of obedience and times of disobedience, and in all he gave thanks for his LORD's protective care in these words penned three thousand years ago.

Remember that you are not like a calf chased by a cowboy God, swirling a rope around your neck and jerking you to the ground and burning your hide with a red hot branding iron. Celebrate that God is your shepherd, carefully planning each day and protecting, providing and guiding you in every detail. Celebrate today that he knows you and loves you, and that you are his glory and pride, since he made you in his image and likeness. Quiet yourself now by repeating throughout the day, "The LORD is my shepherd, I shall not want." Think about that word "shepherd." A shepherd plans the day for his sheep, provides everything they need, and protects them from all enemies. Jesus, our shepherd, does that for us today. Rather than worrying about not getting what you want, or losing what you have, know that your shepherd will supply every need.

Reflect:

We all have misconceptions about God. What kind of wrong images of God do you struggle with? Ask God to quiet you with the idea that he is planning this day for your good, even though you cannot see how that might be. Picture yourself as a little lamb in the arms of the shepherd or as a little child, snuggling in the arms of a loving parent.

DAY 6

The Lord is my shepherd, I **shall** not want.

— Psalm 23:1

We all fear the future. "I shall" describes our attitude toward the future. We live in a fear-filled world. We fear what people might say about us. We fear that we won't have work; and if we do have work, we fear failure and the loss of what we have. We are afraid to be alone. We fear heights or depths. We fear crime. We fear fire. We fear having children. We fear not having children. You name it, and it can inspire fear. What is it like to be free from fear?

At the root of almost all fear is not to know the future. We live in an age of incredible knowledge. No other generation has ever known all that we know today, but one unknowable remains: the future. Even the best of weather forecasters is, at most, moderately reliable.

Back in my college days, when we beat our arch rival in basketball, we always got a "glory day." School shut down for an entire day to celebrate our victory. The fear of losing was erased up by the joy of victory. Before the game, we were anxious about winning, because we did not know what the outcome would be; but on the day after a win, we were joyfully celebrating. We knew the victorious outcome, and our fear was gone. Victory brings relief and joy. Freedom from fear is joy.

The Bible tells us that God can give us a peace that is beyond the "manipulation" of the mind, and a peace that is even greater than the "power of positive thinking." How can he do this? He can do it because he alone knows the future. Paul, in writing to the Philippians, describes that peace in these words: "And the peace of God, which transcends all understanding, will guard your hearts and your minds in Christ Jesus" (Phil. 4:7).

For over forty years I have had the privilege of seeing God at work in India. I am convinced that the main ingredient fueling the awesome reenactment of the book of Acts in India today is the joy that poor people feel in being set free from fear, because they have discovered that their new shepherd, Jesus, supplies everything they need. Life becomes a daily celebration of God's goodness as these new Christians rejoice in their newfound freedom from fear. This is the significance of Jesus' proclaiming that he came to set "prisoners" free (Luke 4:18).

Our shepherd, who is the ultimate source of freedom from fear, does not live in time. He is eternal, beyond time. He is in the future, and we are "in" him. So even though we cannot see what is going to happen in the future, he does, and we know that we are protected by him, because that is one of his promises to his children.

The single greatest problem facing Indians is the fear they have of their idol gods. They live in constant fear of offending one of the 330 million idols that they serve. They believe that to cause offense to these idol gods will bring frightful consequences for them: they will die, only to be reborn to a far lower level of life. It is natural then that they are among the most superstitious people on earth. Gandhi, in his autobiography, called the belief in reincarnation a belief too heavy for any man to bear. Superstition abounds when fearsome beings threaten punishment at every moment of life, and you live in the fear of being born in the future as an outcaste, or even as an animal.

A high-caste Brahmin lady who had recently come to know the LORD stated with joy so great that tears rolled down her face, "You don't know the fear that Brahmins live with each day. Everything we do has the potential to anger the gods. I have such joy knowing that the true God loves me so much that he sacrificed his own Son for me and paid for all my sins. I am free from fear for the first time in my life. Joy floods my heart."

As she said this she began sobbing with joy as she looked up to the heavens. "All of my life I was taught that I had to sacrifice my life for the gods; now I know that there is a God who sacrificed his Son for me. I have all I need in Jesus. Just think — the Creator God of the universe loved me so much that he gave his Son to die for me." She was overwhelmed with joy, and the superstition and fear were gone from her life.

Once, when calling upon an elderly lady a day or two before she passed away, I offered to read Psalm 23 for her. I was surprised at her response: "That won't be necessary, Reverend," she said with an amazingly strong voice. Then, without further words, as she lay in bed with her hands folded over her stomach, she recited the entire Psalm for me in a strong, confident voice. Psalm 23 freed her from the fear of dying. In her darkest moment before death, she knew that she had all she needed to face the future.

Reflect:

What are some of your deepest fears about the future? How does turning to Jesus wash these fears away?

DAY 7

The Lord is my shepherd, I shall **not want.**

—Psalm 23:1

We live in an age of *want* or self-gratification. Six to ten commercials a show interrupt TV programs every five minutes, fanning our desires to get more stuff. Screeching several decibels above the normal program sound level, the commercials tell us that if we buy this expensive swimming suit we will join the tanned and handsome people having a glorious time on a sunny beach—beautiful people who seem afraid of nothing. Such people don't exist, of course. That swim suit will do it all for us. Just getting it will take all our fears away. If it is not a swim suit, it may be another piece of clothing, or a car, or a new hair style or color.

The irritatingly high volume of the commercials will supposedly insure that we will listen to this "important" message and be moved to "want" yet one more, often unnecessary and unneeded, thing. What does the promise, "I shall not want," have to do with this constant fanning of our so-called needs? How can the right soft drink ensure great peace, or the right beer fill us with happiness and joy, or the newest car provide us with lasting thrills and excitement? Can stuff set us free? We are afraid that we won't be able to acquire this stuff. But even if we do acquire it, we then become afraid that we will lose it.

What do the words, "not want" mean? Is all desire wrong? Must we give up wanting things as the Buddhists do? What about all the Bible promises that if we are faithful, we will be prosper-ous? How do all the trials and troubles of life fit in with this promise of "not wanting" or "not lacking" anything?

To "not want" is different than having a quiet life. The apostle Paul tells us that we are at war: "For our struggle is not against flesh and blood, but against the rulers, against the authorities, against the powers of this dark world and against the spiritual forces of evil in the heavenly realms" (Ephesians 6:12-13). Those with great courage are not hampered by fear. To "not want" means that we have more than enough to win; there is no doubt that we have the victory.

Bible stories are almost always about trouble. Elijah didn't have a quiet and tranquil life fighting King Ahab. For three years he ran for his life. Just when he settled nicely at the brook Cherith and was fed by ravens, the birds stopped bringing food, and the water dried up. Certainly he must have wondered what God was doing when God moved him out of Israel to the widow of Zarephath, who was collecting sticks for her last meal before she and her only son believed that they would starve to death. What good could this poor widow do for him? Yet God commanded him to ask her for food. In it all God provided, and Elijah gained the great victory, standing alone against all the idolatrous priests of his day. Elijah never "wanted" for sustenance. God supplied all that he needed to win the victory, but not necessarily all that he wanted to be comfortable.

How did God preserve the Jerusalem church? He did it in the context of persecution. Read Acts 8:1-4: "On that day a great persecution broke out against all the church at Jerusalem, and all except the apostles were scattered throughout Judea and Samaria... Those who had been scattered preached the word wherever they went." One would expect the early Christians to have been crippled with fear, having lost their homes and businesses. Just the opposite was true. They were filled with peace and joy. Wherever they went, they shared their joy in Jesus, their shepherd. God used that persecution to move the Christians from their contented clustering in Jerusalem and instead scattered them all over the area. We want to live quiet and tranquil lives, but in this world of sin, those kinds of lives can be deadly.

If we are not free from persecution or trials, from what then are we free? We are assured that we have all we need to become victors over our trials. We are free, because we have everything we need to face our problems and to come out the victors. We are no longer weak and without resources, for Christ is in us. Are we experiencing trouble? Our shepherd will provide everything we need to overcome the trouble. He will use the trouble to grow us in our trust and confidence in him. God sees our needs, not in terms of temporal gifts, but in terms of preparing us for eternity.

While traveling through the garden valley of California, lined on one side by majestic, snow-capped mountains, I was grumbling and complaining about everything that was wrong in my ministry. My companion who was driving the car interrupted me and said, "John, see those beautiful mountains? How many tomatoes are grown up there on the mountain tops?"

Jesus, our shepherd, supplies all we need, wherever we need it, but especially when we are in the valleys.

Reflect:

What valleys have you gone through? What spiritual needs were met in them for which you can give thanks today?

WRAP-UP

With your group or family, share your experiences of being set free from fear.

- Share with each other what belonging to your family has meant. Give practical examples of something that happened that made you feel you belonged.
- What was the most frightening experience you had in growing up?
- When did you feel most lonely?
- What was the most important experience of belonging to Jesus you have ever experienced?
- What words of the Psalm connected the most with you in this section?

Review the Words:

- *The:* What is *the* source of freedom from fear for you? Explain.

- *LORD:* Who is he in your life?

  The Lord is my All in All

- *Is:* Does he really set you free from fear? Are you "in" him? Most often I can experince God's hand on mine in times of fear

- *My:* How does this little word help you conquer fear? To know that I can claim God as my Sheperd is huge. He sees ME

- *Shepherd:* What does this word mean to you in terms of alleviating fear?

  The word Shepherd just gives comfort & care!

- *I shall:* How does this verse help you face the future? To remember Gods constant eyes on me makes be free of fear for the future

- *Not want:* Who knows what you need?

  Get out of the drivers seat & let God be God, His plans for me are perfect.

53

Provision

```
He makes me lie down in
     green pastures,
  he leads me beside
   quiet waters...
```

— Psalm 23:2

We need peace, and verse 2 shows how a shepherd provides peace for his sheep by leading them to secure places and making certain that they are free from fear, friction, and flies and that they are supplied with food. Jesus gives the peace that is beyond the power of positive thinking or the manipulation of the mind. As we begin to understand what's involved in "green pastures and quiet waters," we will experience some of that mysterious peace. We will discover new ways to overcome our fears.

DAY 8

He makes me lie down in
green pastures,
he leads me beside
quiet waters...

—Psalm 23:2

Constantly in the throes of life's circumstances, distractions, and trials, we must remember just who our shepherd is. He is our Lord and our protector.

Sheep are some of the most unusual of animals. Most animals can fend for themselves. Sheep cannot. Left alone in a rocky area, they have no ability to find grass. A shepherd must guide them to the grass. Even when the shepherd guides them to a green pasture, they are often rebellious and stray far away. When predators attack them, their only defense seems to be to run, which never works well. Wolves and wild dogs can decimate a herd of sheep in just one night, because they don't know how to protect themselves.

In many ways we are like sheep, helpless and defenseless. We can be so proud, so self-sufficient, so certain of ourselves. But it can all be taken away in a moment. My fishing on the Gulf of Mexico was interrupted one day by a strange, grey cloud in my left eye. I could not see through it. It happened quietly, so quietly that I did not notice it at first. I thought a speck of dirt was irritating my eye, but I soon found out that it was more than a speck of dirt; it was a tiny blood clot. The clot did its damage, and in 24 hours, I lost most of the vision in that eye. No doctor could prevent it from happening or restore my lost vision. I was defenseless and helpless.

But God did provide in a host of ways by meeting all my needs in this very sudden and unexpected situation. Life is filled with these kinds of experiences, all of which arouse immediate fears. I was afraid of going blind. Would this vision loss stop with just one eye? God was testing me. Did I really believe that he would provide?

Frankly I had doubts at first, as all of us occasionally will. "God, what will happen if you take my sight away? How will I serve you?" Fortunately a series of "strange coincidences" started to occur. Of course, these were not coincidences, but were God's beautiful answers to prayer. God provided in his own special way, and while I did lose some of the sight in one eye, my peripheral vision was saved.

I think of Jacob, one of Mission India's workers in India who was arrested by terrorists. He was a South Indian working in the North where South Indians are not welcome. The terrorists captured him and made Jacob dig his own grave; since people in that area are not laid down in the grave, but are buried standing up, the hole he dug had to be very deep. He stood on the edge of his grave, and as the terrorists raised their guns to shoot him, he prayed, "Jesus, I am not done serving you. I have a little two-year-old daughter who needs me. You are my protector, and if you want me to stay, please keep these men from killing me."

Jacob said that at that moment an awesome, powerful Spirit fell on the terrorists, and the leader suddenly said, "Don't shoot. Move on." The terror-ists silently lowered their guns and moved out. Jacob told me that it was the greatest gift God had given him. He now knew who his "shepherd" was and had experienced the amazing, supernatural power protecting him. He said that he would never be the same.

I am like a sheep, prone to take the wrong direction and unable to find that which really satisfies and feeds me. I am so helpless compared to him. How much I need him. It is he, not I, who provides all that I need.

The two men who wrote in the beautiful Heidelberg Catechism statement that our only comfort comes from belonging to our faithful Savior (recall reading #1) also wrote this beautiful statement of how our shepherd, Jesus, cares for us. They described God's care as:

> The almighty and ever present power of
>
> God by which he upholds, as with his hand,
>
> heaven and earth and all creatures, and
>
> so rules them that leaf and blade, rain and

drought, fruitful and lean years, food and drink, health and sickness, prosperity and poverty—all things, in fact, come to us not by chance but from his fatherly hand.

Whenever I am afraid, I turn to Job 38:4 and celebrate the fact that "he" is in control, not I. He did not ask me for my advice in creating and controlling it all. "Where were you when I laid the earth's foundation? Tell me, if you understand?" Any being that can be described in those words is qualified to be our shepherd. We need to celebrate *him* today, seeing our smallness and finiteness and reflecting on his greatness. *He* is the one who will make us lie down in green pastures. *He* will find the quiet waters. *He* will restore our soul. We need to trust *him.*

Reflect:

Are you afraid because of something that has just happened? Remember, he has the answer to each challenge of the day. You are not "his advisor." Remember it is he, not you that controls your life.

DAY 9

He **makes me** lie down in
green pastures,
he leads me beside
quiet waters...

—Psalm 23:2

We have two boys and two girls. God gave the four of them to us in just five years. You can probably understand why we believed in putting them to bed early each night when they were all between two and seven years of age. We were probably more motivated by concern for our need for rest than theirs; at the very least, Mom and Dad longed for the rest.

But we had a problem. We lived in Michigan, and in June, on daylight savings time, it is still light at 10:00 P.M. Just imagine four active children longingly looking down each night from their bedroom windows and seeing their playmates happily playing in broad daylight. We are still reminded of our "cruelty" in making them go to bed at 7:00 o'clock each night.

"Making" children go to bed can be a big problem, both for parents and for the children. Some kids have temper tantrums. Others will not sleep until Mom climbs in bed with them, or Dad reads a story to them. There are thousands of excuses that our creative little ones can invent to justify why they should not go to bed. Making children go to bed is difficult to say the least.

I remember Sunday afternoons as a young boy growing up in a very conservative family that strictly forbade any form of Sunday labor. Mom and Dad *made* us take naps each Sunday afternoon. I thought, "If heaven is eternal rest, and God makes me take a nap forever, I certainly don't care to go there." What is there to celebrate in the phrase "makes me"? None of us like to be forced to do something.

Philip Keller, in his classic book on the 23rd Psalm, gives a beautiful answer to this concern. He says that there are four things that prevent sheep from lying down and resting, and a shepherd has to address each of these: fear, friction, flies, and food. Making sheep lie down involves removing the fear, fighting, and flies and providing food for them.

As long as sheep fear some nearby enemy, they will not lie down. Keller points out that sheep are so fearful that even a wild jack rabbit will make a sheep bolt, and then the others will follow in panic. When we are afraid, even though we might lie down, we will still toss and turn. Fear makes us sleepless. Keller said that nothing quieted his sheep more than his presence as their shepherd.

My wife and I have found that the presence of Jesus does the same thing for us when we focus our thoughts on him. One morning, at about 3:00 A.M., I was awakened by my wife's singing, "Jesus, Jesus, there's just something about that name." We were staying in a parsonage in England while I was on a speaking tour of five cities. I had spoken on prayer that day. Whenever she sings this song, especially late at night, I know that fear has kept her awake. That night she felt a horrible demonic presence in our room. She turned her mind to the

Good Shepherd who promises us freedom from fear forever. As she softly sang her praise, he quieted her heart and her fear fled. He "made" her lie down. She has often called on the name of Jesus to quiet her fears, both in singing that little song and in the words of her prayers.

Keller also states that friction and fighting in the herd will hinder the sheep from lying down. The shepherd "makes" the sheep stop quarreling and fighting. When people hurt us in any form, we tend to lay awake, mulling it over and over and getting ourselves all worked up. Sleep escapes us. Only Jesus our shepherd can remove this problem; if we focus our thoughts on him, rather than on savoring hurts and rejections, he will bring us peace and give us rest. I often wake around 3:00 AM. When I do, I fill my mind with the words and teachings of Jesus. Books are born at these times; sermons are written in my mind. But I must confess that some negative thoughts and worries still creep in occasionally. Then I ask Jesus to please take over all my worries. I find that when I really do release my worries to him, as he asks me to do, he gives me peace and rest. "Cast all your anxiety on him because he cares for you" (I Pet. 5:7). He "makes us lie down."

Then there are flies biting, irritating, and burning the sheep. These are all the little irritating things of the day, which at night can become so major, so utterly blown out of proportion that they keep us awake. When seen in the light of Jesus, they suddenly lose their overblown importance and melt away. Jesus can "make us" be quiet. He can make us fearless.

Lack of food can also keep the sheep awake. They will not lie down as long as they need something to eat. Spiritual hunger is one of the major reasons for our sleeplessness. One of the best ways to quiet that hunger is by singing as many familiar hymns as you can recall. Our Shepherd chases flies away, quiets fears and frictions, feeds our spirits, and fills us with his peace.

Reflect:

What is troubling you today? Give it to Jesus and let him worry about it. He is your shepherd, and he knows what you need. He can MAKE you lie down.

DAY 10

He makes me **lie down** in
green pastures,
he leads me beside
quiet waters...

—Psalm 23:2

People often view Hinduism as a peaceful religion. That is hardly the case. Hinduism breeds fatalism, and fatalism breeds fear. Hindus believe in reincarnation. This means that the 330 million gods in which Hindus believe determine, upon your death, in what state you shall be reborn. This decision is based upon what you have done in your previous lives, and the cumulative record determines what you are born to be in this life. There is nothing you can do to change that.

If you try to improve yourself, you may anger the gods and be born to an even lower state in your next life. You can do nothing to move beyond the social status decreed by the gods as a result of your previous lives. Gandhi, in his autobiography, called reincarnation a burden too great for any person to bear. According to a Barna, poll, over 25% of Americans have traded their belief in the resurrection for the fatalistic, fear-fostering theory of reincarnation.

Consider what this means if you are an untouchable or an outcaste—if you are someone who has no status or caste at all. If you are homeless, you believe that you are merely getting what you deserve; you obviously sinned badly in previous lives and deserve to sleep on the streets. You believe that you are only receiving the just reward for your sins. When you beg in order to stay alive, you may be affording someone an opportunity to do a good deed, but you do this at your own risk. Thus, beggars never say "thank you." They are the ones doing the service and risking the anger of the gods by allowing you to help them. While it is good to help beggars, it is not good for beggars to receive that help; for in receiving that help, they are not accepting their just punishment. Thus, when you beg, you never need thank someone for helping you, because you are the one taking the risk by asking for relief from the decree of the gods.

Women at the bottom of the social scale are often treated as being subhuman. Cows are considered to be of more value than a *dalit* or untouchable woman. Mission India targets these women by training indigenous Indian missionaries to teach them to read and write using Bible-based primers. As the women come to understand that they are not subhuman, but instead are really image bearers of the God who created them, freedom from fear and the peace that passes all understanding floods their entire being and spills over into their families. These people, delivered from the horrible caste system, know how to "lie down" with their shepherd, Jesus, caring for them. Imagine the transformation they go through from believing that they are subhuman to knowing and trusting that the creator of the universe is their savior and their shepherd.

This knowledge is the source of perfect peace.

Knowing that God, the creator of the universe is caring for me allows me to lie down in "green pastures." How many of us go through life deeply troubled because we are not okay with ourselves? We are too fat, or too dumb, or our nose is too big, or we make mistakes all the time. We are constantly at war with ourselves.

We don't understand the wonder of "lying down" in the love of Christ. I think of the incredibly intimate relationship that we have with Jesus, as described by Paul: "And we know that in all things God works for the good of those who love him, who have been called according to his purpose...He who did not spare his own Son, but gave him up for us all—how will he not also, along with him, graciously give us all things?" (Rom. 8:28, 32).

When I am down and depressed, I remind myself of my relationship with my Savior. The New Testament says that we are his bride (Rev. 21:2), his body (1 Cor. 6:15), his branches (John 15:1-5), and the building in which his Spirit dwells (1 Cor. 6:19).

In addition to the magnificent honor of being

called Christ's bride, body, branches, and building is the beautiful picture found in Zephaniah of being a little baby held in a parent's arms. In Zephaniah 3:16 God tells us not to let our hands hang limp, since the LORD our God is with us, and he is mighty to save us. Celebrate that glorious fact today. Let your heart sing with joy for what God has made you to be. You may consider yourself a failure, but God doesn't. "He will take great delight in you, he will quiet you with his love, he will rejoice over you with singing" (Zeph. 3:17).

Knowing our relationship to our shepherd brings the deepest, most wonderful peace we can have. Picture yourself holding a little child in your arms and singing softly. Your heart is bursting with joy as you look down at your precious little one. You sing quietly, comforting the little miracle cuddled in your arms. That is a picture of your relationship to the Father in heaven. Right now he holds you in his arms and is softly singing in joy over you. Lie down now. Go quietly to sleep. Rest in Jesus.

Reflect:

How does the marvelous fact that you are tenderly held in the arms of the Savior as his child impact your fears today? What fears is he taking from you?

Rev 21:2 - We Are like a bride
dressed for her husband
I Cor, 6:15 - we live knowing that
Our bodies belong to Christ.
John 15: 4-5 God is the vine
And we Are the branches, we
live because we Are Attached
to the vine
I Cor 6:19 Our bodies Are
where the Holy Spirit lives.

DAY 11

He makes me lie down in
green pastures,
he leads me beside
quiet waters...

—Psalm 23:2

Our shepherd makes us "lie down" by giving us freedom from fear, freedom from fighting, freedom from pesky flies, and freedom from hunger for food. That lying down is the peace that comes when we know that Christ defends us against all evil, and that when evil comes, he will turn it out for our good. The "green pastures" we think about today encompasses all these things.

When we think of sheep, we often think of rolling green meadows dotted with hundreds of little white sheep grazing contentedly without a shepherd in sight. However, this picture could never happen in the Mideast, the area where David kept his sheep, nor could it happen in India. In India one never finds sheep without a shepherd, for the land is barren, brown, rock-filled, and burning under a relentless equator sun. It is filled with enemies of sheep. They can never be left alone. These barren deserts picture where we end up when we wander away from God. Sheep end up in barren places unless they have a shepherd to lead them to the "green pastures."

What are "green pastures"? There are two types of green pastures described by George Smith in his book, *Four Psalms*. As you look over the barren wilderness, you find two breaks in the monotony. Both contain shade, providing escape from the burning sun. There are the deep and dark ravines and caves in which wild animals hide. Sheep stumbling into these ravines are in constant danger of being attacked. They need a shepherd to guide and protect them. The second group of dark areas is the shaded sides of small hills, where, in the protection of trees and large boulders, often a gentle spring bubbles up, or a quiet stream runs. Sheep cannot find these places by themselves. They need a shepherd who knows the way to guide them there. Once there, their fears are removed, the friction among them ceases, the flies are driven away, and they eat the fresh grass, often in the morning when it is wet with dew.

A third kind of "green pastures," described by Phillip Keller in his book, *A Shepherd Looks at Psalm 23*, are little plots of grass planted by the shepherd in shaded areas to make grazing plots for the sheep. These plots are very difficult to start and to maintain. Stones and debris must first be cleared, the land must be tilled, and seed must be planted and watered.

In all kinds of "green pastures," however, there is nourishment. The sheep are fed "new" grass, not old, stiff, dry grass with little food value. Sheep are led to the pastures of newly sprouted grass in the spring, and it is here that the little lambs can reach 100 pounds in 100 days by foraging on the knee-deep, tender, new grass.

In Matthew 18:3 Jesus tells us that in order to enter the kingdom of heaven adults must be converted to become like little children. In effect, there is a sign hanging over heaven's door that says, "No adults admitted." Unless we become as dependent and trusting as a little three-year-old child, we cannot enter. Little children are helpless, totally dependent on their parents and guardians. They are easily lost and quickly excited. They do not know what nourishing food is. But most important of all, they must trust their parents for everything. In that sense, they are like sheep trusting their shepherd for all their needs.

When we have reached the point of trusting Jesus as little children trust their parents or guardians, we will have entered the "green pastures of peace," having safely come out of the "wilderness of fear." The Psalm builds up to this point very quickly by starting with what literally translates, "My shepherd is shepherding me." Do we believe this—that Jesus is guiding us each moment? He knows where the shady ravines are that cast the welcome shadows and provide fresh water. He knows where he has planted those periods in our life in which he will nourish and grow us spiritually, often through dark days. The dark spots in our life are those carefully groomed green pastures or little ravines along the brook, producing rich, spiritual fruit. In these times we have no choice but to cease the frantic running of our lives and the busy rat race that keeps us from looking to Jesus. When trouble comes, bringing life to a screeching halt, we scream at the LORD, "Why are you doing this?"

The answer is simply, "I am getting you out of the burning sun into the shade to experience my tender care." Is Jesus saying to you, "Let me worry about the problem now…you, my little child, need to go to sleep." The hymn says it so well: "What a friend we have in Jesus, all our sins and grief to bear." Yet, how seldom it is that we do fully trust him, choosing instead to cling to our fears, to our fights, and to our flies.

Reflect:

Daily fears surround us. How do the words "green pastures" help you face these daily fears?

Just to KNOW the Lord is my Shepherd, gives me a true peace, He makes me lie down, lends me beside still water, AND He restores my soul.

DAY 12

He makes me lie down in
green pastures,
he leads me beside
quiet waters...

—Psalm 23:2

Our word for today is "leads." In this Psalm it is surrounded by two other little words; it is wrapped up
in "he" and "me." Let's look at the entire phrase "he
leads me." *He* of course is the Creator. "*Me*" refers to
the creature the Creator created. The relationship
binding us to the God of the universe—the Creator
of all things, the God who has no beginning and no
end—is the word "leads." God did not merely create everything and let it spin out. He leads us, his
creatures, day-by-day, as a loving shepherd leads
his sheep. Can you imagine being led by the God
who created the universe, and can you imagine
that leading extending into every incident of your

daily life? How differently Jesus looks at our lives than we do, for he sees them from the perspective of eternity. He is not blinded by temporal desires. He knows eternal values and how often they contradict what we want.

Isaiah tells us that God leads us by holding hands with us. "This is what God the LORD says—he who created the heavens and stretched them out, who spread out the earth and all that comes out of it, who gives breath to its people, and life to those who walk on it; I, the LORD, have called you in righteousness; I will take hold of your hand" (Isa. 42:5-6).

God's description of himself is awesome here:

- He is the LORD of all,
- He is the one who created the heavens,
- He "spread out" the earth and everything in it,
- He gives life to all living beings, and
- He has called us in righteousness.

He is our shepherd, and he is not leading us randomly. He tells us that he has a plan for each of us. "For I know the plans I have for you," declares the LORD, "plans to prosper you and not to harm you, plans to give you hope and a future. Then you will call upon me and come and pray to me, and I will listen to you" (Jer. 29:11-12). This is the work of a shepherd who does not lead his sheep randomly, but leads them according to a daily plan he has worked out.

In Ephesians 2:10 we are described as God's workmanship: "For we are God's workmanship, created in Christ Jesus to do good works, which God prepared in advance for us to do." Before we were ever born, God had a detailed plan for each of us concerning the flow of *his* goodness through our good works.

Each day the shepherds in the Middle East planned where and how to lead their flock to grass and water. In that rocky, dusty, dry area grass and water were not available as they are in many areas of New Zealand, Europe, and the United States. Much thought and care went into planning for the welfare of the sheep. Set yourself free from anxiety today by concentrating on God's leading.

Remind yourself that Jesus, not you, has planned each moment of your day. Quiet yourself in trust and listen carefully for those impulses directing you to do the good God has planned for you to do before you were born. Be excited in anticipating the Master's guidance.

Isaiah pictures God's guidance in terms of a parent holding a child's hand. Imagine you are holding the tiny hand of a two-year-old child as you are walking together. The child is at perfect peace, delighted and content. Mommy, Daddy or a beloved friend is near, holding that tiny hand. Celebrate today that the Creator is holding your hand. (Read Isaiah 42:5-6.)

I remember the time I first held the hands of our grandchildren. Free from the pressure of having four children to care for in just five years, the grandchildren received a bit more unhurried care and reflection than had their parents. I remember their little blond heads as those tiny hands were held in ours, and we wondered, as we walked with them, what God had planned for them.

But these precious little grandchildren didn't

always hold our hands. One of those little boys refused to do so, because he was so full of energy and happiness that he just had to skip! He just could not walk as slow as grandma and grandpa did. Life for him was a constant dance. He seldom walked; he was always skipping and bouncing along. His joy in living had to be expressed by skipping. Another one was far too curious to walk quietly along the path in the woods, holding our hands. He was off on constant excursions to the side of the path looking for salamanders under rotten logs. I remember one walk when, in one hour, he excitedly found over fifty of the ugly little black things.

The picture of little ones walking with us, or dancing ahead of us, or wandering off to the side of us, exploring the wonders of creation are all pictures for us today. "God leads his dear children along." Our shepherd knows where the quiet waters are and how to get us there and place us quietly beside them.

Be quiet today.

Reflect:
Picture yourself either holding Jesus' hand, or dancing before him, or exploring alongside him, as you walk together throughout this day.

DAY 13

He makes me lie down in
green pastures,
he leads me **beside**
quiet waters...

—Psalm 23:2

What thoughts does the word "*beside*" invoke in this context? The word "beauty" comes to mind. Jesus, leading us beside quiet waters, means that when we walk with him, we walk beside beauty. Walking with Jesus blesses us with a beautiful tranquility.

Water has a way of quieting us if it is still, but not stagnant. When David uses the words "quiet waters," we are taken to a quiet stream or a small bubbling spring that is surrounded by the fresh, tender, grass that is so desperately needed by the sheep. He is not referring to the waves of a tsunami or the roaring turbulence of a hurricane. When John tells us in Revelation 21:1 that there is no more sea in heaven, he didn't mean water. The sea for the Jewish people was a dreaded symbol of turbulence and death. The quiet water David speaks of here is the refreshment of a spring or small stream.

I've spent most of my life in what is popularly known as the "water state": Michigan. Many people do not realize that Michigan is the heart of America's fresh water supply. Composed of two massive peninsulas laid between the Great Lakes, the state has more miles of shoreline than the entire Eastern Seaboard. With over 20,000 lakes and 38,000 miles of trout streams, anyone not impressed with the magnificent scenery of Lake Michigan or Lake Huron can turn inward to an almost unending panorama of tranquil beauty in the inland lakes and rivers. The Upper Peninsula alone has over 150 picturesque waterfalls.

It is not just water in liquid form that is beautiful. Snow and ice can present their own pictures of "silent beauty." I remember a day trip to the Upper Peninsula to visit the Tahquamenon Falls. I've referred to it before in other writings. It had been foggy the night before and the temperature dropped far below freezing. All the little droplets of moisture froze into sparkling diamonds clinging to the rusty barbed wire fences, transforming them into things of beauty. The thirty- and forty-foot pine trees surrounding the Tahquamenon Falls were bowed low with foot-high drifts of snow resting on the green boughs of the pines.

We climbed down below the falls that day (no longer possible) to see an amazing frozen waterfall displaying all the colors of the rainbow. I will never forget that moment as I prayed, "God, you know that if we could even create something like this, we would be charging admission to see it. But you do it every year—amazing us with this massive, stunning waterfall each winter, and you don't even charge admission to enjoy it! And then you melt it and send the water thundering down into spring, then summer, and on to the brilliant colors of fall, only then to refreeze it for another year."

What a wonder to be "beside" the still waters, be they liquid or snow. Sheep grazing in fresh grass, then, lying down beside quiet, fresh, pure, gentle streams of water present a beautiful, peaceful scene. No matter where one lives, all people can imagine this beauty. It is the beauty of being with Jesus, the Savior, the one who created all the beauty in the universe. He went beyond that to give his life for us to ensure through that sacrifice and resurrection that his eternal life is ours; we shall live forever with him!

Wrap up all the scenes of quiet water, from the little streams in the desert to the thousands of miles of rivers and coastline. Put it all together. Imagine the beauty. Rest; be quiet; observe Christ's splendor all around you. Realize that the author of all of this gave his life for *you*.

Reflect:

Walk today "beside" the beauty Jesus places in your life. Observe the flowers and birds and tranquil garden scenes today. Then look at an even greater beauty as you imagine yourself beside the quiet waters of your favorite place. Think of the beauty of Jesus, your shepherd, who cares for you, leads you moment-by-moment, gives you eternal life, and loves you with a love that has no limit. Be free from fear.

DAY 14

He makes me lie down in
green pastures,
he leads me beside
quiet waters...

—Psalm 23:2

We've seen the security in the scene this verse depicts as our shepherd Jesus leads us on the planned path of our lives, while we tenderly hold his hand, or dance with joy. While never far from his presence, we explore the wonders of his creation. We've surveyed the beauty of the scenes that are beside the still, quiet, tranquil lakes and streams. We've considered the beauty of snow and ice. In our last look at this glorious picture, we walked by quiet waters.

Water also reminds us of a thirst that needs quenching. We live in what the prophet Ezekiel described as a "dry and thirsty land" (Eze.19:13).

Phillip Keller points out that thirsty sheep are restless sheep. In our frantic world of consumerism, materialism, secularism, and individualism, there is no finding the quiet water that satisfies for eternity. Our world today is not a quiet one. Even though we are told that a certain brand of beer will give us happiness or a soda will give us true satisfaction, these are lies. They do not provide the quiet for which all our souls are longing.

Thousands of years ago the prophets were warning God's people about the danger of drinking bad water from cracked wells that not only do not quench thirst, but also poison and bring death. "My people have committed two sins: They have forsaken me, the spring of living water, and have dug their own cisterns, broken cisterns that cannot hold water" (Jer. 2:13).

On their way to the "quiet waters" sheep will often be distracted by stagnant, poisonous waters; without the careful watch of the shepherd, they can drink themselves to death. We live in the age of drinking poisoned waters; our lives are filled with suffering people, restlessly seeking to satisfy their thirst at dirty, broken, stagnating cisterns.

In contrast, Christ, our shepherd, offers this: "Everyone who drinks this water will be thirsty again, but whoever drinks the water I give him will never thirst. Indeed the water I give him will become in him a spring of water welling up to eternal life" (John 4:13-14).

I think of Abdul, a convert from Islam, living in Bhopal, India. Upon deciding to follow Jesus, his father took his photography studio from him; his brothers beat him, cracking his knee cap with a rod; and his Imam pronounced a death warrant on him. One would think that under such pressure anyone would reverse his decision to follow Jesus, but not Abdul. His story is told in a Mission India video and concludes with the picture of his wife, his children, and Abdul smiling from ear to ear. Abdul says, "I have found true happiness and peace. I am one hundred times happier than I have ever been. No, I am a thousand times happier."

In our frantic search to find satisfaction in ever more "new" consumer goods, we drink from cracked wells into which the poison of selfishness seeps. Only when we give ourselves to Jesus and keep our eyes fixed on the beauty of his infinite love for us, will our thirst be quenched, the restlessness gone, and that refreshing quietness found.

Recall John 4:13-14, and note the strange statement that when we drink "living water" from Christ, it will bubble up, becoming a stream of "living water." When we drink living water, not only is our thirst quenched, but it also starts a spring flowing. We become the head waters of rivers of living water flowing from us, making the dry, brown landscape green with eternal life. Through faith in Jesus, we drink the water of life—the result is a never-ending stream of eternal life flowing from us, out to the world.

Jesus used the vision of the "leaky temple" found in Ezekiel 47 to describe everyone who believes in him. If you read the book *Why Give?* you will remember that the vision of the increasing stream flowing from the temple is really one more picture of God, the God who pours out upon

WRAP-UP

With your group or family, review the seven reasons for freedom from fear that we studied in this section.

Review the Words:

1. *He:* Who has been leading you lately? How were you led? What happened? *Remembering who He is, is key. Keep my eyes on Him.*

2. *Makes me:* Did he "force" you to slow down? Is there any special way in which he set you free from fear? *Sometimes God does slow me down, to "hear" Him. When I give Him control I'm free from fear.*

3. *Lie down:* Was there any point recently in which your restlessness vanished, and you were quiet? If so, please describe. *Lots of times. I my quiet times I feel the presence of God*

4. *Green pastures:* What are some of the green pastures to which God has led you? What impact have they had on leading you out of fear?

5. *Leads:* Did you feel at any time that you could say, "I'm holding hands with God?"

Every day

6. *Beside:* Have you been more observant of the beauty around you lately? If so, what did it do to quiet your fears? *The beauty of nature always makes me stand in awe, but I have to slow down to*

7. *Quiet waters:* Is your restlessness gone? *see it.*

Which of these words gave you the most freedom from fear? Share your experiences.

Leads

Restoration

He restores my soul.
He guides me in paths of
righteousness
for his name's sake

—Psalm 23:3

In verse 3 David talks about restoration to wholeness. Paul speaks about a "mystery of God's will" in Ephesians 1. Even though all the king's horses and all the king's men could not put Humpty Dumpty together again, Jesus is able to put us back together again. Our shepherd, Jesus, brings us back together in love. God is putting everything in the universe back together again. Upon restoration to a right relationship with God through Jesus Christ, we enter the supernatural world of freedom from fear.

DAY 15

He **restores** my soul.
He guides me in paths
of righteousness for
his name's sake.

—Psalm 23:3

There are three scenes that illustrate the significance of this verse: The first is that of lying on our backs, paralyzed and filled with fear; the second is Christ raising us up; the third is walking with the Savior and our loved ones and participating in all the activities of our family and friends. Being surrounded by loved ones, with Christ at the center, is what heaven is all about.

Once again we turn to Philip Keller's, *A Shepherd Looks at Psalm 23*. (I strongly recommend that you get a copy of his book and read it. Over a million copies have been sold. It is also available in a delightful children's edition.)

Keller points out that one of the major problems that a shepherd can face is a "cast" sheep. Occasionally a sheep, while lying down on its side, will roll over into a hollow spot on the ground and end up on its back with its feet straight up in the air. Once in that position, sheep cannot roll back over and get up. The sheep bleats and kicks its legs in the air, all to no avail, and if it is not found swiftly by the shepherd, it will die. The word "restore" as used in shepherding refers to saving a "cast" sheep by helping it stand and walk again.

Jesus may have been referring to cast sheep in his parable of the one lost sheep. Ninety-nine were safe in the fold, but one was missing. Such a sheep would be lying helplessly on its back, kicking and bleating, so the shepherd, leaving the flock in safety, would hurry out to find it. Upon finding the sheep, the shepherd would massage its legs to get the blood circulating and then gently roll it over and make it stand. Even then, it would still be wobbly, and the shepherd might lift it, put it over his shoulders, and carry it home to a celebration (Luke 15:1-7).

A cast sheep is in a fearful state, stuck on its back, alone, and apart from the flock. Our worlds are filled with people just like that. Overwhelmed by life's problems, they feel alone and lost, waiting for someone to find them. It is the picture of modern society, being alone, helpless, isolated from each other, and filled with fear.

Even a noted atheist acknowledges the positive impact that churches have in gathering people together. In *Religion for Atheists: A Non-Believers Guide to the Uses of Religion*, the author, Alain de Botton, has some unique advice: "Religions seem to know a great deal about our loneliness. Even if we believe very little of what they tell us about the afterlife or the supernatural origins of their doctrines, we can nevertheless admire their understanding of what separates us from strangers and their attempts to melt away one or two of the prejudices that normally prevent us from building connections with others." He goes on to suggest that atheists should start up restaurants that require their patrons to sit with strangers and discuss topics suggested in the menus. The greatest problem of modern society is loneliness and its accompanying fear.

Loneliness is fed by hyper-individualism, which in turn is fed by selfish consumerism. "Shop 'til you drop," goes the mantra. The economy depends on sales. We are promised that recessions will be cured when buying increases. The government does all it can to get people to begin buying again. We rejoice when the consumer index rises. It means "better days" are here again and more jobs are available.

Unfortunately, such consumerism feeds and breeds individualism. Individualism feeds and breeds loneliness, which in turn breeds fear. Let's face it, society for the most part measures success in material terms. How big is your house? How new is your car? What does "getting ahead" mean if not that it is measured by the amount of "stuff" that is acquired and not by knowing and enjoy-ing the comfort of friends and family? We are a lonely, fear-filled people living like cast sheep, full of anxiety and feeling forsaken. T.S. Eliot described modern society as "a thousand lost golf balls and a thousand lonely miles of asphalt."

Jesus, the Good Shepherd, is restoring us from being "cast down," lying in loneliness and fear. A most precious human treasure is community. Even atheists acknowledge that they need it. Christ provides it, now and for eternity. Jesus is gathering his "cast sheep" and bringing them safely into the eternal peace and joy of his "flock." Are you experiencing that transformation?

Reflect:

What impact do your family and your friends have on dispelling fear in your life and in bringing joy and happiness? Are you part of a small circle of Christian friends who support each other, share with each other, and pray for each other's needs?

DAY 16

He restores **my soul**.
He guides me in paths
of righteousness for
his name's sake.

— Psalm 23:3

Esther knew only loneliness as a dwarf living in India. Because of Esther's dwarfism, her family and the villagers believed that the gods had cursed her. Every time someone looked at her, they were reminded of the curse and were afraid that by even looking at her, the same gods might curse their children. Esther rarely ventured out of the family home. She preferred the security of her parents' love to the stares and snide comments of the neighbors. Esther's parents also preferred that she stay home. They, too, believed that she was cursed by the gods, even though they loved her.

One day Indian evangelists, who were trained by

Mission India to teach the illiterate poor how to read and write, put on a skit in the village to motivate people to join a literacy class. It would meet five evenings a week for a year. Those who joined would learn to read and write on a fifth-grade level. They also would learn about diet, hygiene, and income generation. Esther's parents watched the skit, and though they had not allowed Esther to go to school, they did allow her to go to the literacy class.

The literacy class teacher, a Christian, embraced Esther with love and acceptance and instructed the class members to do the same. For the first time in her life, Esther experienced acceptance by people other than her parents and siblings. The love of Christ, through the teacher and the class, laid the foundation for the "restoration of her soul."

One of the lessons was about a little man named Zacchaeus who was very much like a dwarf (Luke 19:2). Standing in the crowd, he was too small to see Jesus, so he climbed a tree. Esther was touched by the way Jesus stopped, looked up in the tree, and told Zacchaeus to climb down, because he wanted to go to his house that day.

Esther was amazed that Jesus wanted to eat in the home of a little man, when he could have gone to the leaders' homes instead.

"What a wonderful God Jesus is," she exclaimed. "Jesus even loves little people. He wanted to go to Zacchaeus' house. He wanted to eat with that little man." Because of this story Esther gave her life to Jesus and became his committed disciple. The fear of rejection by others was gone, replaced by the wonderful knowledge that Jesus loves little people and does not believe that they are cursed. Esther began a life of celebrating this phrase: "He restores my soul." She became an ardent follower of the Good Shepherd who loves "little people" like her. She was set free in her "soul" by the knowledge that Jesus did not see her as being someone who had been cursed by the gods because of her size.

Her new love for Jesus and Jesus' love for her radiated from her whole being. Her sparkling eyes, exuberance for life, and her tender care for her parents led them to follow Jesus as well. And as her parents also had their "souls restored," their joy spread throughout the entire village. The villagers who once believed Esther to be the gods' curse now found her to be an exceptional example of the love of Christ. A church was formed to celebrate the freedom from fear given to his followers by the Good Shepherd.

The meaning of "restores my soul" must be seen in the context of the shepherd saving the "cast" sheep in the Middle East. It is simply the return of a solitary "cast down" sheep into the safety of the flock. It is the taking of a lonely, isolated person into the love of Christ and the love of his community.

God created us in his image, and that image is the image of three Persons in one being. The mystery of the Trinity should not overwhelm us to such an extent that we don't even try to ponder it. The Trinity—the Father, Son and Holy Spirit—are the ultimate picture of perfect relationships, and we have been created in that image and likeness (Genesis 1:26-27). The Bible tells us that God is love. That can only be true if there is more than one person to be loved within that being called God. It takes two or more for love to exist. A solitary individual can love only himself, and that is not love, but rather is selfishness and narcissism.

At creation, God referred to himself in the first-person plural: "Let us make man in our image and our likeness" (Gen. 1:26). He was not talking about one individual. God created us as spirit beings with bodies, to live in love relationships with him and with each other.

When we read that the Good Shepherd restores our souls, it means that he picks us up and returns us into a relationship of love with God and with one another. It is that love that works supernatural transformation, healing the deep scars of rejection. Just as the Triune God belongs "together" as Father, Son, and Holy Spirit, so our deepest need is to belong to him and to each other, for we are created in his likeness—for this love to be absent is against our very nature.

Reflect:

Share your ideas about the meaning of "my soul."
Why is "freedom from fear" similar to "freedom from loneliness?"

DAY 17

He restores my soul.
He **guides** me in paths
of righteousness for
his name's sake.

—Psalm 23:3

Sheep don't know where they are going. Left alone they follow the same path and dig it into an ugly rut, eventually ruining the entire area. Lacking any inclination to forage, they over-graze and strip a pasture bare of food. Sheep do the same thing over and over and are unable to move on without a guide. They remind me of one of the "rules" of some churches: "We *never* do anything here for the first time."

King David was well aware of the foolishness and the inability of sheep to forage properly or to protect themselves. They need guides to lead them and protect them. When David wrote, "He guides me," was he thinking of his own wandering, willful life? The Bible is amazingly compelling as it paints real pictures of the saints, not whitewashing their sins away. I wonder if David was older as he wrote, reflecting on his adultery with Bathsheba and the murder of her husband, Uriah. Did he see the mess he made, both in that incident, and perhaps in other areas as well?

Charlie was our Indian guide for our Mission India tour groups for many years. A jolly man with a constant stream of jokes, he was able to keep the attention of the group more than any other guide we had. But I was always surprised at the number of people in a tour group who would travel over ten thousand miles to see India, yet who would not even give Charlie their attention. They always found something more interesting to do than listening to his description of the Taj Mahal or of some other ancient wonder. Wandering around, talking to each other, they missed most of what Charlie had to say. Some other place, removed from the group, seemed more interesting to them. Leading tour groups to India over the years has convinced me that many people are like sheep; they are hard to herd.

In order to follow a guide, you need to have three things: commitment, concentration, and closeness. These three things are all expressions of trust. If we trust someone, we will be committed to concentrate on what that person tells us, and we will want to stay close to him or her. Do you want Jesus to be your guide? It all begins with trust, and trust means commitment to what he says, concentration on what he says, and closeness to him so you can hear him in spite of the distracting noise around you.

Commitment requires concentration. When following a tour guide, there are hundreds of things clamoring for one's attention, and it is so easy to wander off, distracted by something that appears to be more interesting. Isn't it that way in our relationship to Jesus? We need to commit to concentrating on where Jesus is leading. To follow our guide, we need to listen for his guidance. Listening also requires us to respond to his leading with immediate action. The following anecdote illustrates this.

A young mother with four excited little children came into the McDonald's restaurant where my wife and I were having coffee one afternoon. It was a very small McDonald's, and we could not help but notice the children. A young boy about ten was the oldest, accompanied by his younger brother and two noisy, even younger sisters.

Watching them made both my wife and me think back to when our family of four children, two boys and two girls, all born within five years, were also very young. We, too, would come into a McDonalds just like this mother, with our own two little boys and two little girls; and we'd struggle to keep them under control.

As we watched, my wife said exactly what I had been thinking: "We should pay her bill." I immediately took out a twenty dollar bill, and my wife brought it up to the counter and gave it to the mother, saying, "Here, we'd like to pay for you." The mother looked startled. "I've already paid," she said. My wife replied, "Well then use it for the next time."

The mother was about to cry as she said, "Thank you so much. This is my oldest son's birthday party. I'm so grateful." We thought back to those days when we brought in our excited gang of four with the strict orders that they could each spend only one dollar, which of course bought a lot more then than it does now, but it still required them to choose carefully, and with limits.

So why did both of us have the same prompting at the same moment? We believe it came from our guide, God's Spirit, who leads us each day on his paths. His path is always new, always different, always fresh. Every day he gives new promptings which, when acted upon, will bring joy to others. If you are committed, concentrating on recognizing and obeying his promptings and being close to him, you will find him guiding you daily into exciting discoveries and opportunities. We have the greatest guide in the universe, and following him frees us from fear.

Reflect:
When have you felt Jesus prompting you or guiding you to help someone?

DAY 18

He restores my soul.
He guides me in **paths**
of righteousness
for his name's sake.

—Psalm 23:3

Boredom with many traditional church services is a major problem in Western Christianity. For some, it can be that so many things seem more interesting than organ music, ancient hymns, or ill-prepared sermons. There is a deadening apathy that seems to be killing many churches. That apathy is the devil's powerful tool. He has used it for centuries, beginning with the very origin of the church. But Christ still rules, and in the year 2010 the number of churches in the USA stopped declining and actually started to grow again. New, fresh forms of worship are cropping up and attracting tired disciples.

When we walk the same path, over and over

and over, the path will become a rut. As we mentioned earlier, sheep do that; unless guided on different paths, they will wear down the path, cutting it into a deep rut.

We become bored doing the same thing repeatedly, and boredom with Christ is the devil's delight. When the church sinks into saying, "We never do anything for the first time," watch out. Remember, Jesus seldom leads us over the same path repeatedly. The word is paths—path with an "s" on it. "Paths" is plural. Every day is a brand new, exciting path to righteousness, filled with small, but fresh, new surprises.

Read Jesus' words to the church that failed to follow their guide—the church that failed to stay close in an exciting, growing, passionate love for Jesus:

> I know your deeds, that you are neither cold nor hot. I wish you were either one or the other! So, because you are lukewarm—neither hot nor cold—I am about to spit you out of my mouth. You say, "I am rich; I have

acquired wealth and do not need a thing." But you do not realize that you are wretched, pitiful, poor, blind and naked. I counsel you to buy from me gold refined in the fire, so you can become rich; and white clothes to wear, so you can cover your shameful nakedness; and salve to put on your eyes, so you can see (Rev. 3:15-18).

As I write, I think about some of the exciting paths on which God has led my wife, Atts (my wife's full name is Adelaide–we don't know how she received this strange nickname), and me through three pastorates. In our first church, a rural one in the corner of Minnesota, ten miles from Iowa and South Dakota, the LORD guided us to fresh paths. For instance, once we arranged to have thirty African-American children visit from a Chicago inner-city church to spend a week on a farm in Minnesota. For the first time, our community's children were able to meet and interact with people of a culture different from their own.

We enjoyed many exciting experiences following Jesus on this unique path.

It was hard, though, to do evangelism in that little village. So Jesus, our guide, led us with a simple, fresh idea: build a small wayside chapel; place it on the hill north of town, alongside the busy US Route 75. The congregation loved this new, exciting path! It took only six weeks to construct the chapel with its two rows of pews inside and its steeple on the roof. Christian literature and free Bibles were made available to the traveling visitors, and during the subsequent fifty years, hundreds of thousands have stopped to meditate, pray, and take away some literature. Jesus guides along unexpected, but fruitful and exciting paths.

In the second church, we continued to search for a way to witness that was culturally compatible with the congregation and the secular audience of that time (in the late sixties). Again, Jesus led.

I was led to write a simple Bible correspondence course, aimed primarily at those who were unfamiliar with the Bible. I encouraged the congregation to hand out "enrollment cards" offering the course. All that was needed to enroll was to have the potential students put their names and addresses on the cards. They then mailed the card back to us. In the first six months, over 500 people enrolled in the course, and we saw more people come to Christ during that time than in the fifty-year history of the church! Within the next ten years, one million copies of the first book had been distributed by churches working cooperatively in 130 U.S. cities. It was called "Project Philip." (It continues to this day—you can learn more about it at www.projectphilipministries.org.)

Jesus led with the young people of the church in yet another way. At a time when my annual salary was only about $7,500, the young people of our church collected loose change each month by calling on every family in the church, and by doing this, they raised $12,500 in only ten months. Talk about an exciting path!

In the third church, we were introduced to prayer—"morning prayer," as many people turned out every morning at 7:00 A.M. to pray for our missionaries. We met each morning for about twenty-five years. Mission India grew out of that prayer time, and it has become one of the major mission forces in the Spirit's movement across India. Our Savior leads us in ways that are so much greater and so far beyond what we can even imagine on our own! Rejoice that he is leading you and doing through you things you cannot even imagine (Ephesians 3:20).

Reflect:

What new and fresh things has Christ done in your life lately? Explain how your anticipation of these fresh new things of God drives out fear.

DAY 19

He restores my soul.
He guides me in paths
of **righteousness**
for his name's sake.

—Psalm 23:3

For many, the word *righteousness* can have a negative connotation. It is often used to describe some pompous person who is self-righteous. We need to erase that negative feeling about the word *righteousness*. When we are told that Christ guides us on paths of righteousness, he is not speaking of the righteousness of the Pharisees or of any religious leader or person who is self-centered.

One of the best descriptions of righteousness is found in Matthew 25:31-46. Here are some of the paths on which Jesus leads.

When the Son of Man comes in his glory, and all the angels with him, he will sit on his throne in heavenly glory. All the nations will be gathered before him, and he will separate the people one from another as a shepherd separates the sheep from the goats. He will put the sheep on his right and the goats on his left.

Then the King will say to those on his right, "Come, you who are blessed by my Father; take your inheritance, the kingdom prepared for you since the creation of the world. For I was hungry and you gave me something to eat, I was thirsty and you gave me something to drink, I was a stranger and you invited me in, I needed clothes and you clothed me, I was sick and you looked after me, I was in prison and you came to visit me."

Then the righteous will answer him, "Lord, when did we see you hungry and feed you, or thirsty and give you something to drink? When did we see you a stranger and invite you in, or needing clothes and clothe you? When did we see you sick or in prison and go to visit you?"

The King will reply, "I tell you the truth, whatever you did for one of the least of these brothers of mine, you did for me."

Then he will say to those on his left, "Depart from me, you who are cursed, into the eternal fire prepared for the devil and his angels. For I was hungry and you gave me nothing to eat, I was thirsty and you gave me nothing to drink, I was a stranger and you did not invite me in, I needed clothes and you did not clothe me, I was sick and in prison and you did not look after me."

They also will answer, "'Lord, when did we see you hungry or thirsty or a stranger or needing clothes or sick or in prison, and did not help you?"

He will reply, "I tell you the truth,

whatever you did not do for one of the least of these, you did not do for me."

Then they will go away to eternal punishment, but the righteous to eternal life.

Righteousness is found in small acts of compassion and consideration. Righteousness is not some abstract idea, but rather it is the daily expression of kindness and concern for those in need. Righteousness is love for the needy; it is compassion for the hurting. It is honesty and trustworthiness. It is humility and unrewarded love.

Jesus was in opposition to the religious leaders of his day, in a war so intense that it led to his crucifixion. These leaders were power-grabbing Pharisees. They held on to their positions through legalistic enforcement of over 600 regulations. Theirs was a heartless society, filled with constant quarreling and debating over the finer points of some law. Compassion was not a concern for the practicing religious leaders of Jesus' day.

When the disciples saw a man born blind, they argued over whether that man or his parents had sinned. Their attitude betrayed the cold, condemnatory, legalistic wisdom common in that day that insisted that a blind man had to have gotten what he somehow deserved. Their religion lacked warmth, compassion, and, above all, love. Christ rebuked them strongly, saying that neither was true. In fact, this man and his circumstance presented an opportunity for God to show his beauty and his love (see John 9:1-3).

James 1:26-27 presents one of the more concise explanations of "righteousness" to be found in Scripture:

> If anyone considers himself religious and yet does not keep a tight rein on his tongue, he deceives himself and his religion is worthless. Religion that God our Father accepts as pure and faultless is this: to look after orphans and widows in their distress and to keep oneself from being polluted by the world.

Jesus always guides us into this kind of "compassionate righteousness." The greatest law is to love God above all else and to love our neighbor as ourselves. Jesus fulfilled that law for us so that, as we follow him, we are legally covered by his righteousness. Our loving response to this act of grace, and our duty, is to listen daily to his direction, and to express this new compassion and tenderness for those in trouble. Who needs your care, your smile, your little gift, your listening ear, your attention? Jesus is always leading his children on new paths of righteousness–he doesn't lead us on worn-out paths or into a rut or a ravine. Concentrate on looking for his new direction of compassion today.

Self-centered concern breeds fear. Jesus came to set us free from fear. The primary weapon in breaking our slavery to anxiety and worry is to turn our attention to others and devote ourselves to helping them. The moment that becomes the dominant role of our lives, we will be walking on the "paths of righteousness."

The kings and queens of heaven are seldom

recognized here on earth, for they are the "little people" who, without much recognition, have sacrificed themselves in service to others. They know the peace that passes all understanding.

Reflect:

What do you think of when you hear the word "righteous"? Is it positive or negative? How does the practice of loving concern for others drive out fear?

DAY 20

```
He restores my soul.
He guides me in paths
    of righteousness
for his name's sake.
```

—Psalm 23:3

Why concentrate on Jesus? Why try to follow him? What does "his name's sake" mean?

A young couple wanted to join a mega church in our city, so they followed the customary practice of most churches and attended a new member's class. There were about twenty couples in the group, and the pastor started by asking his usual question: "Why do you want to join this church?" The answers he received were the usual ones:

"I like the music here." "The pastor really

has tremendous messages, and I'm

challenged by them." "We have teens, and

we are looking for a place in which they
will feel at home."

On and on went the answers until the pastor
came to one special young couple who startled
him with their answer: "We came because we felt
that we could best serve the LORD here. There are
so many opportunities for service."

The pastor would later recall, "In all my time
asking this question that was the first time I
received that answer. Most new members join
because they feel the church is here to serve them,
and not because the church offers them opportunities to serve others."

Churches tend to be spiritual supermarkets
offering sparkling, attractive programs that entice
people to "buy" in. Two principles guide their
paths: "What can we offer you?" and "How many
people can we get into our *store*?" We attempt to
get people to join for our reasons, not for Jesus'
reasons. Churches compete for members, and
pastors measure success by the number of people
attending worship. Being able to give a large num-

ber in answer to the question, "How many people worship with you?" seems to be the force that drives their actions.

I must confess that both as a pastor and as a mission executive, I, too, have fallen into this trap of numbers. Often I wanted to build my congregations, but Christ's Spirit would in effect say (in a rather loud voice),

"No."

I would reply, "Why not?"

He would say, "Can you build an ear of corn?"

"Of course not," I'd reply.

"Why not?" he'd press.

"Because corn is living," I'd acknowledge.

"What do you think the church is? Living or dead?"

"Living."

And true to his Word, God's Spirit would

conclude, "Then plant seed—the seed of eternal life, my Word. Don't try to build a church; help me to grow it."

Building churches is what we do in human strength. Growing a church is what we do in God's strength through planting and cultivating the spiritual plants springing from God's Word. It is always "his," not "mine." How can there be competition between churches when all belong to him? Yet from the very beginning, the demons have planted division between leaders and their churches, and competition seems to flourish. Pastors often refuse to meet together to pray for each other and the needs of their community.

One of the most shocking moments of my life occurred while reading Isaiah 2:8. "Their land is full of idols; they bow down to the work of their hands, to what their fingers have made." As I meditated on that verse, I was convicted that my congregation and my mission could easily become my idol. I was trying to build the church. Was it the "work of my hands" or was this congregation the result of "plants growing in the life of Christ?" I realized that I was competing with others. I was striving for personal success. Did I want it to be the best, so that I could bow down and worship the "work of my hands," and not the Savior who was leading me?

The drive for personal success is universal in our human nature. People feel the need to be successful. We feed on success. We compare our success to that of others. We get depressed when we come up short or when we fail. We are fearful of failing. Students commit suicide out of fear of not passing a test and falling short of their classmates' achievements and others' expectations for them. Christ gives us escape when he beckons us to follow his paths and not our own. But we often treat our Savior as someone who is disabled, who needs our help; or as some impoverished person whose mission needs our money; or as some disorganized naïve person for whom we need to lay out a plan to help his mission succeed.

We must remember it is he, not we who leads. We walk his paths, not ours. The word for today is *his*, not *mine*. We follow his paths. We recognize that we are sheep, constantly wandering off the path and not knowing where we are going, and so he graciously and lovingly leads us. We cannot lead ourselves. The one who came from heaven and returned to heaven and who sees life from the eternal perspective is our shepherd, leading us on his paths, not ours. Isn't that a relief!

If that doesn't free us from fear and fill us with peace, what will? When will we stop arguing with him? We must surrender to him and be set free from the prison of having to prove that we are successful. Then we can celebrate—we can enjoy traveling with Jesus. He knows that he has already made us successful, so we can relax and surrender our anxieties to him today.

Reflect:

Have you become a prisoner of success? What is your motivation to follow Christ? Are you trying to help him out, or are you letting him guide you in his paths?

DAY 21

He restores my soul.
He guides me in paths
of righteousness
for his **name's sake**.

—Psalm 23:3

Our motive for following Jesus should be clear: he is the ultimate, the only reliable guide. We can try to make it on our own, building our own success, only to have our efforts crash down around us. Even the greatest of world leaders will fall from power eventually. None can make it alone. Jesus alone gives us freedom when we learn how to follow our perfect, all-knowing guide. Once you learn to trust him totally, you will be set free from fear for all the days of your life, and for eternity.

But even more, our motive for following Jesus should be his own desire to be followed. He wants us to do it for "his name's sake." After all, God has identified himself as being the very definition of love (1 John 4:8). Therefore, he wants us to follow him as our response to his infinite love for us. He wants us to love in return, and this love must spill over to all those he places in our paths. He wants us to walk in compassionate righteousness, so that we will be displays of his perfect compassion and love.

Are you thankful for your great guide's love? Do you celebrate him each day? Do you long for others to know his love? Paul, writing to the Colossians, gave us one of the greatest descriptions of the Good Shepherd. Go through these descriptions carefully. In Colossians 1:15-20, meditate on these descriptions of the guide who leads you on his delightful, beautiful, exciting paths to the right life—a life of kindness, love, compassion, and beauty. Your Good Shepherd is:

- "the image of the invisible God" (v. 15);
- "the firstborn over all creation" (v. 15);
- the Creator of all, "for by him all things were created: things in heaven and on earth, visible and invisible, whether

thrones or powers or rulers or authorities; all things were created by him and for him" (v. 16);

- "before all things and in him all things hold together" (v. 17);
- "the head of the body, the church" (v. 18a);
- "the beginning and the first-born from among the dead, so that in everything he might have the supremacy" (v. 18b);
- the fullness of God in human form, "for God was pleased to have all his fullness dwell in him" (v. 19); and
- the reconciliation of "all things, whether things on earth or things in heaven, by making peace through his blood, shed on the cross" (v. 20).

Read and re-read these glorious descriptions of the Good Shepherd that you are following today. Do you doubt that he can whisper to you, prompting you to do the right thing? Do you believe he knows more about the path than you do? Do you think he accomplishes his will, even when you feel burned out and worn down?

Follow him, celebrating him. May the celebration of who he is be your motivation for trusting him to lead you to live in child-like faith—celebrating, dancing, and singing on his beautiful paths through this temporal life, and on into eternal life.

Reflect:

Dwell in your Guide's greatness throughout the day as he sets you free from the fear of not being successful. How does his greatness give you peace?

WRAP-UP

With your group or family, review the seven key words and phrases:

1. *Rest:* What freedom from fear has been given to you, and, in turn, what freedom are you extending to your family, friends, and fellow believers?

2. *My soul:* On what have you been basing your sense of identity and value? How does knowing Jesus loves you make you more secure?

3. *Guides:* What is your reaction to the three actions in following a guide – commitment, concentration, and closeness? When are you practicing these in your response to Jesus?

4. *Paths:* Do you have regular, amazing experiences with Jesus directing you which help you build a sense of peace and confidence in him?

5. *Righteousness:* What has been your understanding of righteousness? Has it changed? How are you practicing righteousness each day?

6. *His:* Is it Christ's name or your name that is driving the way you live your life?

7. *Name's sake:* Why do you want Christ's name to be elevated in your life? What fears has his perfect love conquered in you?

Protection

Even though I walk through
the valley of the shadow
of death, I will fear no evil,
for you are with me; your
rod and your staff,
they comfort me.

－Psalm 23:4

Verse 4 speaks about the ultimate protection. We all walk through the valley of the shadow of death. Jesus is there to guard us. We don't like to think about death, but it is certain that we will one day die bodily. No one except Jesus has gone through death and returned to tell us about it. He shepherds us through this mystery of death.

Even though I walk through the valley of the shadow of death, I will fear no evil, for you are with me; your rod and your staff, they comfort me.

—Psalm 23:4

This verse begins with a startling change. David changes from talking *about* his shepherd to talking *to* his shepherd. He moves from speaking of the shepherd in third person, to speaking to him in the second. He is not only telling others about his shepherd; now he is expressing his love directly to his shepherd.

This is a dividing point. We've spent the first three sections talking *about* Jesus our shepherd. In these final three sections we will be talking *to* our shepherd. This brings up a significant point about prayer. When we pray, are we merely talking about ourselves and our needs in prayer, or do we also talk with our Savior about his desires?

In the prayer Jesus taught us to pray, "The Lord's Prayer," we begin by addressing God's concerns first, before our own. This is the polite way of beginning any conversation, namely, to ask about the welfare of the one with whom we are talking. When we talk to God in prayer, let's remember to express our concern for the hallowing of his name, the coming of his kingdom, and the doing of his will in each of the concerns we bring to him.

So often our comfort and relief are the main focus of our prayers. This verse of the Psalm reminds us that our comfort is secondary. All the inevitable and unavoidable problems of our life are opportunities for God's name to be hallowed. His kingdom shall come, and his will shall be done, even as we go through the valley of suffering.

The valleys through which shepherds led their sheep were always pathways to higher ground. Jesus is our shepherd, leading us through all of our valleys to higher ground.

The words "even though" express two certainties about life. The first certainty is that we will suffer, and we will face trouble. We must expect it. We are at war—spiritual war—and the closer we get to Christ, the more fearful the demonic world becomes. Expect trouble. Expect attacks. Expect tough times. The world of evil spirits is afraid. Let them be afraid, for we are the victors. Jesus publicly humiliated them with his death on the cross.

That leads to the second certainty: "And having disarmed the powers and authorities, he made a public spectacle of them, triumphing over them by the cross" (Col. 2:15). The second certainty is that God will win and turn the evil out for good. Jesus has already defeated them. When we follow our Savior's leading, "even though" there will be tough times, he will turn them out for good.

Remember the account in John 9 of the man born blind? As they passed by him the disciples treated the blind man as the subject of a theological argument, which they brought to Jesus to solve. They asked, "Who sinned, this man or his parents?" It reflected the cold, judgmental, and compassionless attitude of a systematic religion. Such religious people don't care at all about such a man's suffering. All they care about is winning their argument.

Jesus corrected their false theology, saying that the blindness had only one ultimate purpose. "Neither this man nor his parents sinned," said Jesus, "but this happened so that the work of God might be displayed in his life" (John 9:3).

As we enter valleys, we must remember that David acknowledged, "even though." Times in the valley are certain, but being led into a valley does not mean that our shepherd has forsaken us. Jesus is with us, in us, guiding us to hallow the name of his Father, to bring the coming of his kingdom, and to accomplish his will. Christ led the way as he went through his own personal valley on the cross bearing the rejection of his Father and those he died to save. "Even though" he was killed, he rose from the dead, lives and rules today, and is coming again in majesty. Even though you may be filled with fear because of the valley you are currently in, please remember that Jesus is leading you through that valley to the mountain top.

Valleys are like the letter *U*. The bottom of the letter is a valley, a low spot. But when we get to heaven, every *U* of life will be turned upside down, and the bottoms will be on top. The darkness and pain of the cross, the Son's experience of feeling forsaken by the Father to suffer human death, is in reality the highest expression of the beauty and wonder of the love of God. Jesus has experienced the worst of any *even though*. There is no greater love than this.

"Even though" life is filled with valleys, when we get to eternity we will see that these were the points that produced the greatest times of trust and companionship with our shepherd and with one another.

Reflect:

What were some of the major valleys in your life? Can you now see in some of them the "even though" idea—that in spite of the difficulty and pain, great good came from these times? Jesus led you through to higher ground.

DAY 23

Even though **I walk**
through the valley
of the shadow of death,
I will fear no evil, for you
are with me; your rod and your
staff, they comfort me.

—Psalm 23:4

The shortest distance between two points is a straight line. Most people know this. I have a friend who has had serious cancer recur four times. He humorously claims that God, however, doesn't seem to be concerned with taking the shortest distance or with straight lines. My friend admits he is puzzled, though. Why, after so much prayer, does the cancer keep recurring? Can't God just cure it and be done with it? Why not just go straight to the cure? Why this wandering back and forth, with one day up, and the next day down, with one year seemingly cured, and the next year recurring.

Come to think of it, God took forty years to lead Israel through the wilderness. If you traveled in a straight line, you could travel the distance in just a few days. Why does God sometimes seem so slow in responding to our prayers?

The key to understanding verse four of Psalm 23 is the word *walk*. We are walking through the valley. We are not in it forever, but we do not run through valleys, much less fly through them. There is no instant way to get through them. It takes slow walking—walking that often seems two steps forward with one step backward. Walking is hard work, but Isaiah 40:31 assures us that we will not faint when walking.

The valley is not a dead end. We are going through it to reach some higher ground. Phillip Keller says that in shepherding sheep, each year is divided into two periods: the winter when the sheep are safely in the fold, and the summer when they are led through dangerous valleys to the higher mountain ranges where there is fresh grass. The walking David refers to is the walking he often took with his sheep as a young boy, as he gently led them past all the dangers of the trek up the mountains to the green pastures of the spring and summer grass. Here they could lie down, free from the burning summer heat. Here they could find the gentle, quiet headwaters of the spring melt-off of winter snows. But, they had to walk to get there.

The shepherd knows the way, since he has traveled it many times. The sheep do not. They tend to wander off. They do not like the strenuous effort required to make the journey.

In Isaiah 40:31 we find that those who hope and wait on the LORD will renew their strength. Isaiah goes on to say that in hoping and waiting, three things will eventually happen: we will soar like eagles, we will run without growing weary, and we will walk without fainting. Isn't it interesting that fainting is not connected with soaring or running, but it is connected with walking? Spiritual walking requires phenomenal strength. To endure a trial that seems unending is the ultimate test of faith. Prolonged times in the valleys of life can result in spiritual fainting.

Think of Job. He lost everything—even his health. He sat silently in his misery. His friends judged him, telling him there was only one reason for the tragedy that befell him. God was punishing him. They said that his only way out was to confess his sins. Job refused to believe that God was punishing him for some wrong he had done; there had to be another reason for what was happening to him, and the other reason was not for punishment, but instead it was to develop his trust.

The ultimate test of any relationship is trust, especially when we cannot see or understand our current circumstances. Marriage is built on trust, and it is destroyed when that trust is betrayed. Fear breeds on lack of trust, especially lack of trust in the Creator God who made us in his image. The first sin of Adam and Eve was their failure to trust God's command not to eat of the tree of good and evil, lest they die. Trust in God is easy when things go well. But when life is filled with trouble, and trouble does not disappear immediately, trusting God becomes like a precious diamond that we present to him.

King David, the author of this Psalm knew well how to wait and walk slowly. He was taught that early in his life when King Saul was constantly seeking to kill him. David was patient. When opportunities came to kill Saul and end the trial, David refused and instead trusted God to work all things together for good.

God doesn't work on the American plan of "instant everything." Trust God. Trust is your "diamond" of love; trust him even when all evidence of his presence seems to be gone.

Reflect:

Have there been times in your life when God has slowed you down to a walk? What did you learn through these times?

DAY 24

Even though I walk through the valley of **the** **shadow of death**, I will fear no evil, for you are with me; your rod and your staff, they comfort me.

—Psalm 23:4

We were "pinned in," and my wife—who suffers from mild claustrophobia—had had enough. "We have to get out of here. Let's turn back. I cannot stand these walls, and I'm going crazy. What will happen when the sun sets and we are caught in here?"

We had been hiking in Capital Reefs, a national park filled with deep canyons that seemed to lead nowhere. We were told that in the canyon where we were hiking there was an old rusting hulk of a car stranded at the canyon's end, and I wanted to see it. The shadows were lengthening, telling us that sun would soon set; they were frightening both of us, as we wondered what it would be like to be caught in the pitch black darkness of the canyon.

We can ridicule people who are "afraid of their own shadow," but we all know how frightening a shadow can be. On another occasion, my wife and I were hiking near an airfield when suddenly, noiselessly, a giant black shadow fell over us. A stealth bomber, on a practice flight, was landing noiselessly, and its shadow caught us by surprise. For an instant, it terrified us.

As the sheep were routed through the canyons on their way to higher ground they were constantly encountering shadows that made them skittish and upset. Life is that way. Every day there are shadows. What are the shadows over your life right now?

In the state of Orissa, in southeastern India, the shadows of persecution fall darkly on 16 counties (districts). Around 2006, at Christmas, a massive wave of persecution drove tens of thousands of

Christians into hiding and eventually into refugee camps. A pastor hid in the deep jungles with his wife and children, just a few feet from the terrorists who were searching for them. They had nothing to eat or drink. The shadows of fear were heavy and dark all around them. After a few days, they quietly came out of hiding and returned to their church, where in the next month, the pastor baptized more new believers than he had in the previous three years combined.

The reason for this amazing turning to Christ was the way in which the pastor and his family handled the shadows. In place of paralyzing fear, they continued to live their lives with love, concern, and forgiveness flowing forth for those who persecuted them. The people around them recognized this gentle, peace-filled, compassionate, and fearless way of living as being something supernatural. They wondered what God could do this for the pastor and his family, and they wanted to know more about such a God who could so completely dispel the shadows of fear.

There are two ways to look at shadows. Shadows are merely distorted silhouettes and not the real thing. They are warnings. Shadows never harmed anyone. A second way to look at shadows is to know that there would never be a shadow in your life unless there was sunshine behind that which made the shadow. Each dark shadow that falls on us is there, because Christ is shining down on us. It is his light that causes the shadow, which is his warning to us to turn to him.

In the last two months, two college classmates of mine who appeared to be very healthy were suddenly translated into heaven, and the "shadow of death" hangs heavy over our lives right now. The last one, who died suddenly three days ago, appeared to us to be in excellent health. We were stunned by his obituary in the paper. In the past year, seven of our friends have been left alone as widows. "Even though we walk through the valley of the shadow of death, we will fear no evil." Every one of us will sooner or later find ourselves in this valley.

Remember the sunshine behind the shadow of death. Without that sunshine, everything would be totally black, as it was for three hours that day 2,000 years ago, when the sun hid its face. Our Savior suffered the blackness of the total absence of the Father, and he cried in agony, "My God, my God why have you forsaken me." But behind those three hours of darkness, the sunlight of the Father's love was shining. And then the darkness faded, and the curtain in the temple was torn apart, so that the glory of the LORD could shine through in a new way. Yes, that sunshine of the presence of God was behind what caused the shadows, and those shadows still bring fear. Just remember that they are shadows, and not total darkness, and shadows exist because there is sunshine behind them. Shadows make us afraid, but when we understand that they are signs of light, they can also be used to bring us freedom from fear.

Reflect:

What are the common shadows that you face daily? What shadow would you fear? How does the idea that these shadows are caused by the light of Christ shining on your problems, set you free from fear?

DAY 25

Even though I walk through the valley of the shadow of death, **I will fear no evil**, are with me; your rod and your staff, they comfort me.

—Psalm 23:4

We know that shadows are caused by sunshine, not darkness. They are not things to fear, but are warnings to get our attention. Once we understand that behind every shadow there is sunshine, we can move on to being free from fear, following the direction of the shadow to find the light.

The focus of this reading is the heart of Psalm 23: "I will fear no evil." That statement is a treasure beyond all other treasures. As Christ's light removes one shadow after another, day after day, we come closer and closer to the full realization of this phrase. "I will fear no evil" is as close to a description of the eternal paradise that awaits Christ's followers as one can get.

The story of one couple that suffered profound loss in the 2004 Indian Ocean tsunami, which struck South India the day after Christmas, helps us grasp the significance of the words "I will fear no evil." The couple was walking the beach near Pondicherry in southern India that morning—they had been celebrating the birth of our Savior with their extended family. Relatives had come up from Kerala, the southernmost state in India, to be with them for a week. Suddenly a massive wave swept over the beach, and nine of their relatives and their three children became part of over 230,000 causalities caused by this massive, natural disaster. They alone were left alive.

The shadow of death hung heavily over them in those moments as they crawled out to dry land and then in vain sought to find their children and relatives. We can hardly bear to imagine the human reaction one would have to such a great loss. But this amazing couple traced the shadow of death back to the "light" and found Jesus there. And in his light, they understood that they were the ones left behind, while their three children, along with their relatives, were singing and rejoicing with music such as has never been heard on earth. They were celebrating with Christ his victory over evil. They were in the land where no one fears or suffers pain anymore.

In the horrible aftermath of the tragedy, this couple became one of Mission India's main forces in expressing the sunshine of the love of Christ to others who had been devastated by the loss of loved ones. Mission India provided thousands of large relief packets, weighing over fifty pounds each, which contained much needed supplies that had been purchased locally to ensure that they would be used. Each time they placed one of the huge packets with a grief-stricken family who had lost all their possessions, they listened to the story of pain and fear told by the recipients, and then they shared their own personal joy about finding sunshine in the midst of this dark storm. Their sunshine was Jesus and the knowledge that their three children and their relatives were now living in the glory and brilliance of his presence. They had been delivered from fear forever.

President Bill Clinton toured the disaster-stricken area and heard about this amazing couple. He asked to meet them, and he sat with them for nearly a half hour listening to their story of knowing peace and joy in the aftermath of losing everything. He came away shaking his head and saying that in all his life he had never met anyone like these two people. His testimony was reported all over India.

The world seems to be teetering on the cliff of economic disaster at this moment. Millions have lost their homes in foreclosures. Never have our streets seen so many homeless. At this moment it is estimated that in my middle-class county of Kent County, Michigan there are at least 2,000 homeless boys and girls. What fear must they have as they bounce from shelter to shelter or end up spending the night in the back seat of a car?

I think of the simple, daily-existence fears of a girl born into a poor family in India. Her father must "buy" a place for her by "buying" a husband with a dowry. If he fails to provide a suitable dowry, he will be totally dishonored in his community. The dowry must increase in proportion to the wealth of the groom's family; merely providing the payment at the time of the wedding is never enough. The groom's mother demands a continuous stream of gifts. In some situations, the mother-in-law may actually set the bride on fire and kill her (called bride burning) in order to free her son to find another wife with another dowry. It is estimated that at least two brides may be burned daily in Delhi alone. Few of us can imagine the fears these young girls have as they live with the knowledge that when they are 12 or 13 years old, they may have to leave their secure family homes for the rest of their lives. We must get the Good News out that by following our shadows to the source of sunshine, Jesus, and laying our fears before him, we can have a peace that is beyond anything we can dream. We must generously share that knowledge with the world.

Reflect:
What do you fear the most? What is your reaction to tracing the shadows of fear to the light causing the shadows, namely, to Jesus?

DAY 26

Even though I walk through
the valley of the
shadow of death, I will fear
no evil, **for you are
with me**; your rod and your
staff, they comfort me.

—Psalm 23:4

Shadows tell us that the sun is still shining. Shadows are caused by blocked sunlight. We can find the sun by peering behind the shadows and seeing the bright light. The question today is: "Just where is the Son who is the Light of the world? What blocks the light, causing the shadows?"

I vividly remember when the answer to this important question first hit me. I was flying to the United States West Coast to address a missionary convocation, and I was fighting depression. I opened the Bible to Psalm 27 and started to read, but could not get beyond the opening phrase in verse 1: "The LORD is my light." The question kept popping up in my mind, "Where is this light?"

I answered it by saying, "LORD, you are shining down on me." And the question persisted in my mind, "Where is this light, John?" And I replied, "I don't get it. You are shining on me, LORD. So you aren't up there shining down on me. Maybe that's not right. Are you right here beside me, shining on me?"

The question continued to haunt me. I remembered that little poem about the footprints in the sand. There were two sets of footprints visible, until trouble came. Then, just one set was visible. "Did you leave me alone then, LORD?" the poem's author asked.

And Jesus replied, "When you saw only one set of footprints, it was then that I carried you." "There," I thought, "I have it. Jesus is carrying me." But that answer didn't help me any more than did the others. Jesus was not shining down on me, or sitting next to me, shining on me, or even carrying me.

"Where is the light John?" I could not shake the question.

Finally the light dawned on me. The light was inside me. Suddenly my fears were gone; my depression crumbled as this brilliant ray of spiritual light penetrated the shadows of my fear and depression and brought me peace and joy. Jesus, through his Holy Spirit, lives in me right now. His light isn't out there, shining in; it is inside of me, shining out. I was dumbfounded. Why had I never seen this before? Why was I always hiding in the shadows when the sunshine was right here in me?

It was the beginning of a new understanding, both of where Christ dwells and of the consequences of this wonderful truth. David only touched on this when he said, "You are with me." The New Testament understanding of it goes further and says, "You are in me."

I immediately began to think in terms of pictures. The picture of two houses came to mind— Mt. Vernon, which I had recently visited, and the White House. Mt. Vernon was George Washington's home, now changed into a marvelously restored museum. As beautiful as it is, and as important a site in my nation's history as it is, it isn't important enough to be the primary target of a terrorist attack. The target terrorists would pick would be the White House. Why? What is the difference? The difference is that the White House is occupied by the most important person in our nation, the President of the United States. Mt. Vernon is unoccupied.

I thought of myself. Am I an empty museum, or does someone live in my spirit? Who am I? Am I merely someone born overweight who has always struggled with a lousy self image and consequent depression? Or do I have, dwelling in my spirit, the Creator of the universe? The thought staggered me. Am I God's White House? Am I the temple of the Holy Spirit? I immediately thought of Galatians 2:20: "I have been crucified with Christ and I no longer live, but Christ lives in me. The life I live in the body, I live by faith in the Son of God, who loved me and gave himself for me."

Here is the key to conquering fear. Christ is in me through his Spirit. I am a branch on the vine of Christ, living in his life (John 15:1, 5). Who is Jesus?

He is the one who disarmed the entire host of demonic powers and authorities. He made a public spectacle of them among the heavenly hosts when he gained the victory over them on the cross of Calvary (Col. 2:15). No wonder David could exclaim, under the inspiration of the Spirit that he would not fear, because God was with him. God is with us in the wonderful, overwhelming sense that he is IN us now. His victorious, eternal, never-ending, perfect righteousness has been planted in us. To be born again means that God's Spirit takes up residence in our souls, and it empowers us to live the life Christ has called us to live!

We do not have to look far to find the sunshine causing the shadows. That sunshine is in us. Fear closes the shades and keeps it from shining out. But when we realize where Jesus is, when we trust that the Light of the world dwells in us, we have the most powerful weapon against all fear. We are living in the impenetrable life of Christ. He is the Victory over sin, death, and the grave. Hallelujah!

Reflect:

What impact does the concept that Christ dwells in you have on that which you fear right now? Explain.

DAY 27

Even though I walk through the valley of the shadow of death, I will fear no evil, for you are with me; **your rod and your staff, they comfort me.**

—Psalm 23:4

The phrase "your rod and your staff, they comfort me" is difficult to understand, since few of us are familiar with the functions of the shepherd's rod and staff. And since we don't know what they are, we cannot relate to the important way in which they are the two fear-banishing weapons in the shepherd's arsenal.

Think of two words which are familiar to us in our culture as substitutes: the "rod" would be a gun, and the staff would be a safety net. The rod is the weapon the shepherd uses to keep outside enemies away. The staff is the tool the shepherd uses to rescue the sheep from their own natural foolishness when they wander away and get into trouble. Thus, we have protection from external enemies and from our own natural weaknesses.

What attacks come from the outside? All saints seem plagued by illness, which is the most common attack. Is illness what Jesus protects us from? While Christ still works supernaturally in the physical world, we must remember that all physical miracles are only temporary. We all face physical death. Every healing lasts only a few years. The majority of us do not experience supernatural healing from our serious, life-threatening physical problems. Joni Erickson Tada became a quadriplegic after a tragic accident. God took that tragedy and turned it into a blessing for millions of people through the faith and courage displayed by this beautiful woman—something that never could have happened, had a physical miracle of healing occurred.

The promise of protection found in the word "rod" applies to a far greater need than merely escape from physical danger and illness. It applies to the spiritual realm. Paul reminds us in his letter to the Ephesians, "For our struggle is not against flesh and blood, but against the rulers, against the authorities, against the powers of this dark world and against the spiritual forces of evil in the heavenly realms" (6:12).

All we need do is call upon the name, Jesus, and the forces of darkness in the "middle" world scatter. It is one of the best kept secrets in Western Christianity, but not in the developing world. One of the reasons the church in India is growing at such an incredible rate is simply because they know something we don't know. They know that there is a spirit world of fallen angels who bind us in dark, deceit-filled spiritual prisons. Indian Christians, for the most part, know that until we bind these prison guards by using the name of Jesus, their stronghold will not be broken, and the prisoners will not be set free. In his second letter to the Corinthians, Paul similarly wrote, "The weapons we fight with are not the weapons of the world. On the contrary, they have divine power to demolish strongholds" (10:4).

My wife and I have been married over fifty years. On one occasion especially, we were arguing so intensely that we stopped talking to each other for two days. We both were furious with the other. One night we resolved to kneel together and ask Jesus for help. As we mentioned his name, an amazing feeling came over both of us. We looked at one another and, in relief, started to laugh. Jesus, our shepherd, threw his "rod" or club at the demonic spirits that had bound us. It was truly a moment of divine, miraculous protection. We did not throw a club. We did not even address our enemies. We trusted Jesus to take care of them. Our enemies are those described by Paul; they are not flesh and blood and those things we see with our eyes.

I think of that little Indian village church where the people were so poor that if they did not work for a day, they could not eat that day. All were "fasting" on Sunday, refraining from all work so that they could worship God. None could read, but all had Bibles. I asked what they did with the Bibles, if they could not read them, and the pastor replied that they opened them at night and spread them on their chests in the belief that the demons would not be able to penetrate this defense. The illiterate villagers were probably more aware of the comfort of Jesus' rod than we are.

Using Jesus' name sends fear to the demonic world. The name of Jesus is the ultimate form of protection. We all need to use it much more often. The name of Jesus is our comfort, the supernatural weapon which guards us. We cannot scare away demonic powers, but Jesus can. His name is our "rod," our weapon. Jesus promises us the power to bind evil powers on earth, and as we do it in his name, he will bind them in heaven (see Matt. 18:18). We are guarded by a weapon of supernatural power—the name of Jesus. Are you using it? Do you know the peace it can bring?

Reflect:

Are you aware of the REAL enemy we face and the protection against it that Jesus gives us through the use of his name? What experiences can you share to encourage someone else?

DAY 28

Even though I walk through
the valley of the
shadow of death, I will fear
no evil, for you are with me;
your rod and your **staff,**
they **comfort me.**

—Psalm 23:4

Someone once said, "We have met the enemy, and he is us." While the shepherd's rod, which is the name of Jesus, protects us from the external attacks, what protects us from our natural tendency to wander off into sin? How can we be so stupid? Why is it that we are so possessed with selfish desires that we can completely fail to see or totally disregard the effects our actions have on those we love? How can we be so inconsiderate, so demanding, so insensitive?

Jesus knows our weakness because he became human, just like we are. He faced every one of our temptations. He knows our struggles and our pain. "For we do not have a high priest who is unable to sympathize with our weaknesses, but we have one who has been tempted in every way, just as we are—yet was without sin" (Heb. 4:15).

I think the single greatest source of fear comes when we face our sins, our weaknesses, and our failures. In a success-driven culture, all of us are failures in one area or another, and often in many! We know it, but we live in a constant struggle to cover it up. We need to impress others. More, we desperately need to impress ourselves. As we lie to others, we lie to ourselves. And we are afraid.

The best illustration of this struggle is found in the parable of the prodigal son found in Luke 15:11-31. Take a moment to look it up and read it before you go on. Think about the insensitivity that is on display in this parable. The wayward son was so callous that he demanded his share of his father's estate before his father had even died. Caring nothing about how he was hurting his father, he went off and wasted everything his father had worked so hard to provide for him. The young son was fooling himself, and it took his having to face starvation to awaken him to his selfish foolishness and cause him to think of his father. But even when he thought of his father, he was not first of all concerned for him, but instead remained primarily concerned for himself. He recognized that his loving father was his only hope. So he decided that in order to save his own life, he must go home and ask his father for a servant's position. It was this decision to ask for a servant's position that was the turning point in his life. There was no more demanding, just humble asking. He was throwing himself upon his father's love and mercy.

There is some evidence that this story was not original with Jesus, but that the Pharisees often told it, but with a dramatically different ending. In their version, the father harshly and, according to them, justly rejected his son and turned him out. When Jesus told the familiar story, he gave it an amazing new ending. The father did not turn the son away with a typically-legalistic, unfeeling rejection. Instead, while the son was still far away, the father picked up his robes and ran to greet, embrace, and welcome him home. There are two amazing things to note here. The first is that this happened while the son was "far away." Jesus did not picture the son as having to prove himself first, before forgiveness was given. The second point to note is the eagerness of the father to forgive his son. He did something no Pharisee would ever have done. He picked up his robes and ran. He lost all his dignity in his eagerness to welcome his son back home.

The story ends with the second prodigal son, the righteous son. This son, too, was deceiving himself by telling himself that he was good. His goodness was purely external. He lacked the internal character to see the goodness of his father displayed by the loving mercy he showed to his younger son. His eyes, as were his younger brother's eyes, were focused only on himself.

God's forgiveness frees us from looking at ourselves with the constant spiritual cancer of our fear of failure. We admit failure. And then we understand that God the Father accepts us without our need to overcome our failures first. He runs to us with open arms at that very moment when we admit our failures. And he can do that, because Jesus not only saves us from our external enemies, but also from our internal enemy, our sins. He washes us. He makes us presentable. He clothes us in his righteousness.

Recall from verse 3 how our shepherd leads us in paths of righteousness for his name's sake. Now meditate for some time on Isaiah 1:18: "Though your sins are like scarlet, they shall be as white as snow."

Remember where Jesus is? He is in you through his Holy Spirit. Christ's Spirit is sinless. There is no worry or fear about the need to achieve success for those who realize that they have been born again spiritually, and that the new life that is now in them is Christ's sinless life. No one can fully understand physical life. The birth of a little child is a great miracle. Far greater is the second birth to Christ's life within us. Understanding who we are in Christ is the single greatest weapon we have to banish fear from our lives: "And the peace of God, which transcends all understanding, will guard your hearts and your minds in Christ Jesus" (Phil. 4:7).

Reflect:

Freedom from fear is that kind of peace that is beyond understanding. It is even beyond "positive thinking." It is the realization that we can receive the gift of perfection in his sight, of being washed as white as snow. Ask God for it today.

WRAP-UP

With your group or family, review the seven key words and phrases:

1. *Even though:* Life has two inevitable facts. Trouble will come. Jesus will lead you through it. How did this realization affect you?

2. *Walk through:* Are you afraid of walking? What is Christ's promise concerning going slowly? (Isa. 40:31).

3. *Shadow of death:* What are shadows?

4. *I will fear no evil:* Have your shadows led you to Jesus, and have you found freedom from fear in his light? Explain.

5. *You are with me:* If someone asked you where Jesus is, how would you answer, and how would that answer free you from fear?

6. *Your rod:* What is the rod Christ uses today to set you free from demonic attack?

7. *And your staff comfort me:* Share with someone any feeling of peace you have recently had.

Victory

You prepare a table before
me in the presence of
my enemies. You anoint my
head with oil; my cup overflows

—Psalm 23:5

To follow Jesus means that his power flows into us and his authority crowns us. The Indian Christians understand Christ's power, especially over demons and their demonic strongholds. The excitement and wonder of experiencing repeated victories over demonic powers, through the power of Christ, drives the spontaneous growth of the Indian church in perhaps the greatest spread of the gospel in history.

DAY 29

You prepare a table before
me in the presence of
my enemies. You anoint my
head with oil; my cup overflows.

—Psalm 23:5

We have reached the climax of the Psalm in verses 5 and 6. Verse 5 is difficult to understand at first glance, as it is written in figurative shepherd-terms. We will be referring to Philip Keller's book again as he explains these shepherd-pictures. But the meaning of the verse goes far beyond David's poem and his shepherd-symbolism; it invokes New Testament pictures of wedding celebrations and eternal feasts. Jesus is leading us to victory. Let us follow him.

In the opening line we will consider four "freedom-from-fear" concepts:

- the person or servant who prepares the victory party ("You"),
- the great victory party ("a table"),
- the person for whom this party is being planned ("before me"), and
- the great defeat of our enemies ("in the presence of my enemies").

Then, in the second line, we will consider:

- being healed of our battle scars ("you anoint my head"), and
- being empowered by the Spirit ("with oil").

Finally, the last phrase is the epitome of freedom from fear ("my cup overflows").

In this reading, let's consider the significance of the shepherd (the "You") who prepares the way for his sheep. Mesa Verde, the site of one of the United States' national parks, is Spanish for "green tableland." It is a huge plateau, high in the mountains, with several excellent remains of ancient cliff dwellings. David refers to "green tablelands" in this verse, according to Philip Keller. The shepherd leads his sheep through the valleys in late spring, winding his way up the mountains to those fresh, grass-filled plateaus. He prepares these plateaus by carefully examining the grazing areas to ensure that all poisonous weeds have been removed, since the sheep will eat almost anything. He also sizes up the area for hiding places for wolves, wild dogs, and all other enemies of the sheep to make certain that they are not lurking on the plateau. He prepares the tableland for the sheep.

Christ is the one who prepares our "table-lands," leading us through our valleys and turning the evil into good as he gradually leads us higher and higher. Who protects us? Who is going before us each day of our lives, ensuring that no poison and no enemies will harm us? Are we responsible to protect ourselves, or is it the Creator and Redeemer of the universe who is responsible?

Paul tells us that in all the rough spots on our journey to that final, eternal feast, God is working all things for good (Rom. 8:28). Trusting Christ to handle each thing that frightens us enables us to find the kind of peace that Paul described as being beyond our understanding and beyond the manipulation of the mind: "And the peace of God, which transcends all understanding, will guard your hearts and your minds in Christ Jesus" (Phil. 4:7).

Peter was a poor fisherman and church planter living along the Bay of Bengal in south India. He was one of the first graduates of our church planter training classes at the time of my visit with him. He had been banished from his village because he was following Jesus. The little church he had planted had almost died. His boat had been taken away from him, and he had no means of support.

My heart was broken as I sat with him and shared his suffering. We prayed. I started to leave, but then he asked me for a gift to buy a new boat. As I was reaching for my wallet to give him the funds, these words came out of my mouth: "No, Peter, you and I will ask Jesus for those funds." I looked around and wondered who had spoken those heartless, words, and I suddenly realized that they had come from me. When I got home, out of guilt for my seeming heartlessness, I made certain that as many of my friends as possible were praying for Peter.

The next year, when I was back in India, I was speaking at a conference of Indian church planters when I saw Peter in the front row. I could hardly wait until I finished speaking to rush up to him and ask him what had happened since I had last seen him. I was amazed at his answer. He had started a number of new little churches during that year. When I asked him if he had gotten a new boat, he seemed surprised by my question. "Of course. Jesus gave me a new boat," he said. We prayed for him to provide, didn't we?" was his answer.

I knew then why those seemingly harsh words had come out of my mouth a year earlier. I had pointed Peter to Jesus as his provider and protector, and not to foreign funds. He knew the true source of his provision. It is God who protects us and provides for us. It is Jesus who turns each evil circumstance for good. Believing that Jesus is our shepherd enables us to live as little children who, when overcome by fear, know where to find comfort—in the arms of a loving parent.

Reflect:

Think about the word "you." Who is the "You" that protects you on the journey through the valleys to the high tablelands?

DAY 30

You **prepare a table** before me in the presence of my enemies. You anoint my head with oil; my cup overflows.

—Psalm 23:5

Who prepares tables in the household of a master? Servants do. Those who prepare a feast for a great dignitary are the servants. Yet David tells us that God, the Creator and Redeemer of all things, is the one preparing an eternal feast for us. God is the servant in this context, and this feast consists of special kinds of spiritual food.

The "table" is a picture of life. Without tables of nourishment we starve. We need to eat to stay alive. Jesus Christ came to prepare an "eternal table" for us. He is our servant, setting out food for us; when we eat this food, we will live for all eternity. It is the food that conquers death. It is the food that satisfies our hunger forever.

Take a look at the table Christ sets before us. See the amazing spread of spiritual food. First there is food that totally eradicates all our sin. Imagine that. All the guilt-driven fears you carry, stemming from all the failures and sins of the past, can be taken away by eating this food. "'Come now, let us reason together' says the LORD. 'Though your sins are like scarlet, they shall be as white as snow; though they are red as crimson, they shall be like wool'" (Isa. 1:18). Spiritual eating is believing, and believing is eating. When we believe Christ died to enable us to be totally forgiven, we are eating spiritual food. Jesus described this at the institution of the last supper: "And he took bread, gave thanks and broke it, and gave it to them, saying, 'This is my body given for you; do this in remembrance of me'" (Luke 22:19).

Christ is sinless. He lives in us. That is the meaning of being "born again." Christ gives us *his* sinless life. The old failures, the guilt, and the ever-present fears suddenly disappear, just as sun breaks through fog, and a believing understanding settles over us. We have Christ's perfect, sinless life in us. Jesus has prepared a table for us. It is filled with sparkling, flawless crystal which contains the perfect drink— the blood of his sacrifice for our sins. What do we have to fear? "If God is for us, who can be against us?" asks Paul in his epistle to the Romans (8:31).

All of us suffer from fears, and those fears come from being separated from God. Fear was the first and the most immediate result of Adam and Eve's sin: "But the LORD God called to the man, 'Where are you?' He answered, 'I heard you in the garden, and I was afraid because I was naked; so I hid'" (Gen. 3:9-10). We are afraid of God, because each one of us knows instinctively that we fall short of him. And as long as we remain separated from the one who is perfect love, our fears cannot be cast out (recall 1 John 4:18).

We try to dispel our own fears. We try to conquer sin by our own means. But that is a hopeless task until we realize that Jesus, our shepherd and our servant, has prepared the food that will totally cleanse us from all our sins—it is the food of his body, his life.

Food not only gives us life, but food also gives us energy. Christ has gone before us not only to give us food that cleanses us from all our sin, but also to give us food that gives us the power to live a productive, meaningful, eternally-successful life. Rick Warren's phenomenally successful books on a "Purpose Driven Life" are a testimony to our fear of failure. We look back on our lives, and we wonder about our purpose, our meaning, and our significance. What have we accomplished that will last? We are so busy with our daily tasks – what has eternal purpose?

Jesus says that the food he puts on our table will not only cleanse us from our past sins, but it will also produce fruit for eternity:

> I am the vine; you are the branches. If a man remains in me and I in him, he will bear much fruit; apart from me you can do nothing. If anyone does not remain in me, he is like a branch that is thrown away and withers; such

branches are picked up, thrown into the fire and burned. If you remain in me and my words remain in you, ask whatever you wish, and it will be given you. This is to my Father's glory, that you bear much fruit, showing yourselves to be my disciples (John 15:5-8).

Paul adds another dimension to our purpose when he states that we will "grow" for eternity into something we cannot begin to imagine: "Now to him who is able to do immeasurably more than all we ask or imagine, according to his power that is at work within us, to him be glory in the church and in Christ Jesus throughout all generations, for ever and ever! Amen" (Eph. 3:20-21). The little acts of love and concern, the sacrifices which are so small that we don't consider them to be sacrifices, all are seeds that Christ grows into eternal and unimaginable significance. C.S. Lewis in his parable, *The Great Divorce,* pictures a large crowd listening to a beautiful woman. The protagonist asks who this beautiful woman is, and an angel replies that she is one of the queens of heaven.

She was from a London slum, "Golder's Green," and a "nobody" on earth. Yet she blessed everyone she met with love and kindness, and her deeds were multiplied beyond anything imaginable.

Reflect:

What seemingly insignificant deeds of goodness do you plant daily? How does it feel to know that all charges against you have been removed?

DAY 31

You prepare a table **before me** in the presence of my enemies. You anoint my head with oil; my cup overflows.

— Psalm 23:5

Freedom from fear comes when you realize that Christ has gone before you to prepare a table of food that gives you a new, sparkling, eternally-sinless life, and another kind of food that makes you produce spiritual fruit, which will multiply for eternity. However, freedom from fear can only be fully realized when you also apply the meaning of the phrase "before me." Jesus has prepared this table before me, or as at a birthday party, *for* me. The significance is that this celebration is for me (for each of us) personally.

Think of your birthday party. Great preparations have been made. You sit down to celebrate.

But where are the guests? You are all alone. It is no celebration, because no one is there to celebrate with you.

The only time Jesus speaks of one sheep is the time that one sheep was lost. The shepherd left the ninety and nine in safety, found the single lost sheep, and brought him back with rejoicing to join the flock. Sheep are always together. So are Christ's followers. We are Christ's disciples, and just as it takes two to be married, so it takes two or more to be a disciple. In no uncertain terms, Jesus made this criteria for discipleship clear: "By this all men will know that you are my disciples, if you love one another" (John 13:35).

One of the greatest problems of Western culture today is the destruction of community and of family. We live in an age of hyper-individualism. We are among the loneliest people of all times. Love corrects that loneliness and is the foundation and cement of relationships. It is in relationships that the image of God in us shines the brightest.

God is three Persons living in perfect harmony: the Father, the Son and the Holy Spirit.

They have never quarreled. They have always existed together in perfect love. They created us in their image, an image of perfect relationships. We were made equals, but different: male and female, so that in our relationships of love with each other, we become "like" the Triune Creator. It is in love relationship with others that we find our individual significance. Significance comes when we "mean something" to those who are around us, when ties of love and friendship are established.

When we sit around a table, we not only picture food, but we also picture relationships. In a famous Norman Rockwell Thanksgiving Day painting, the artist captured the abundance of food present at a feast along with the abundance of love present in family relationships. When David writes God "prepares a table before me," he is referring to a feast of both food and relationships.

Loneliness could almost be a synonym for fear. We are afraid when we are alone. We gain courage when we are together. The idea of "preparing a table before me" involves more than food;

it involves a guest list of loved ones and joy and laughter shared together.

In Luke 14:15-23 Jesus tells the parable of the Great Banquet. The invited guests refused to come, all making excuses. Jesus said that the host insisted on having guests at the banquet, so he instructed his servants to go out into the streets and paths and invite everyone they met. "Bring in the poor and the lame," he instructed them. Still the hall was not filled, so the servants went out into the country lanes. Did Jesus have in mind the vision that was later given to John in Revelation 7:9? "After this I looked and there before me was a great multitude that no one could count, from every nation, tribe, people and language." Remember, when we sit down to the table Jesus is preparing for us, there will be a numberless host of people joining us in an eternal celebration that will destroy all fear forever.

No solider fights alone. No follower of Jesus walks alone. Following Jesus is more than occasional attendance at a mega church, staring at the back of a dozen heads trying to see some spiritual sideshow up in front. So many people think that the reason for going to church is to "get something." We go to church to give something—ourselves. That's how we worship God best, by loving those who commune with us, in love for him. Being born again always involves loving action toward others.

Larry Osborne started his ministry by planting a church in Southern California and worshiping in a rented Seventh Day Adventist church building. A few decades later, North Coast Church has grown to be 23 separate, simultaneous worship centers, involving thousands of church members. The key to this phenomenal growth, explained in Larry's book, *The Sticky Church*, is the small-group-membership requirement made of all the members. Everyone must attend one of the worship centers, take notes on the sermon, and then meet in their small groups on Wednesday night to discuss the practical application of the sermon. People are flocking to this church, for they are finding freedom from their fear and loneliness through the love of their small group members.

Reflect:

How has God used friends and relatives to dispel fear from your life?

DAY 32

You prepare a table before me
**in the presence of
my enemies.** You anoint my
head with oil; my cup overflows.

—Psalm 23:5

We fear enemies. We have good reason to tend not to invite them to our parties. But Jesus makes his table not only in front of us, but also in the presence of our enemies to show us that we have nothing to fear. Why throw a party in the presence of our enemies? What does Christ mean?

Our eternal victory banquet will be in the presence of all who have fought so hard against Christ and his followers. Will our fears be banished and our courage increase so much that our enemies stand helplessly by while we celebrate victory? Who are these enemies who attempt to destroy us? Paul identifies them this way: "For our struggle is not against flesh and blood, but against the rulers, against the authorities, against the powers of this dark world and against the spiritual forces of evil in the heavenly realms" (Eph. 6:12).

Many Western Christians do not realize that we are in a spiritual war in which followers of Jesus are battered, beaten up, and sometimes even killed. Talk to our Indian brothers and sisters, or to our Chinese family members, or to all in the developing world who follow Christ. They know that this war is going on.

We receive weekly accounts of persecution from our Indian workers—reports of unfair treatment in the courts and unlawful imprisonments of believers. Some of our workers have been waiting for trial on trumped up charges for two years. Do you think that God has promised these believers a tranquil and quiet life of prosperity and peace? Christ predicts the opposite for his faithful.

The banquet is being prepared for us, but the celebration feast is not yet ready. The Victory has been won, but the battle has not yet ended. When the time comes for that banquet, all the hosts and allies of the demonic world will be witness to the eternal victory, and their defeat will be known by all. They will see that they did not win, and that we are *more* than conquers. God has defeated evil completely, and the eternal celebration will be held in their presence.

For now, following Jesus is a mixed up experience with times of great peace and joy, followed by times of extreme disturbance. Paul describes it powerfully in his second epistle to the Corinthians.

As servants of God we commend ourselves in every way: in great endurance; in troubles, hardships and distresses; in beatings, imprisonments and riots; in hard work, sleepless nights and hunger; in purity, understanding, patience and kindness; in the Holy Spirit and in sincere love; in truthful speech and in the power of God; with weapons of righteousness in the right hand and in the left; through glory and dishonor, bad report and good report; genuine, yet regarded

as impostors; known, yet regarded
as unknown; dying, and yet we live
on; beaten, and yet not killed; sorrowful,
yet always rejoicing; poor, yet making
many rich; having nothing, and yet
possessing everything (6:4-10).

What does it mean to believe in God, the
Father, the Creator of heaven and earth? The
answer given in the old Heidelberg Catechism,
written in the time of the Reformation, states it
beautifully.

The eternal Father of our Lord Jesus
Christ who out of nothing created
heaven and earth and everything in
them, who still upholds and rules them
by his eternal counsel and providence,
is my God and Father because of Christ
his Son. I trust him so much that I do not
doubt he will provide whatever I need
for body and soul, and he will turn to my
good whatever adversity he sends me
in this sad world. He is able to do this

because he is almighty God; he desires
to do this because he is a faithful Father.

"In the presence of my enemies" means that
God will so over-rule all the evil that is occurring
in your life that it will all be turned out for good.
Your response may well be, "How can that possibly
be? How can God turn this tragedy out for good?
Where can we find any good in it?" My answer
would be simple, "I don't know. I am a small child
when it comes to trying to understand the ways of
my heavenly Father. But I trust him."

I do know one thing. God himself has suffered
the consequences of human evil for the very
purpose of accomplishing our greatest good.
Our heavenly Father allowed Jesus to come into
this world and to suffer the consequences of sin:
death. That is the single, most horribly tragic event
that ever happened in the universe. And if God
the Son is great enough to take upon himself that
evil deed of men, suffering in human flesh the
brutality of crucifixion and death, and turn it into
the greatest good in history, upon which all our
salvation is based, then I am certain that he can

take every one of our tragedies in life and turn them out for good as well. He has proven that he can with his own death and resurrection.

And because he has insured his victory, we can say with Paul: "But thanks be to God, who always leads us in triumphal procession in Christ and through us spreads everywhere the fragrance of the knowledge of him" (2 Cor. 2:14).

So when that great banquet is set before all of us, we will be singing his praises in heavenly songs, for then we will finally see God's victory realized. We will see our lives as he sees them now, from the point of view of eternal values and not from the point of view of our distorted, temporal values. How then can it be anything short of every tear being finally wiped away?

Reflect:

Can you recall a truly bad experience out of which God actually brought about some good? What does this statement "in the presence of my enemies" do when applied to our normal, daily fears?

DAY 33

You prepare a table before me
in the presence of my enemies.
You anoint my head
with oil; my cup overflows.

—Psalm 23:5

Few of us have seen an "anointing" of any kind. To anoint someone with oil is foreign to our culture, but it was very meaningful in David's time. He was anointed as King over Israel by the prophet Samuel, an event that startled everyone and became the major turning point in his entire life. During that long period of persecution by Saul, David's anointing as the next king of Israel provided the patience he needed both to endure his circumstances and to restrain himself from killing Saul on more than one occasion, since Saul, too, was the anointed King of Israel.

The word *anoint* appears many times and is

used in multiple ways in both the Old and New Testaments. In Eastern cultures, it was common to welcome a guest into one's home by anointing him or her with sweet-smelling perfume. Our Western methods of welcoming guests today include a wide range of customs, from giving a hand shake to giving a hug. Not so in Christ's time. Coming in from a dusty trail, guests were greeted with a kiss, their dirty feet were washed, and sweet-smelling oil was placed on the guest's head. Welcoming a guest included embracing, cleansing, and perfuming. It was a beautiful act of elevating the guest into a position of honor.

The Pharisees were constantly trying to trap and condemn Jesus. Chapter 7 of Luke's Gospel recounts how Simon, one of the leaders of the Pharisees, invited the Savior to his home. When Jesus entered the home, Simon snubbed Jesus by refusing to greet him with a kiss, or to wash his feet, or especially, to anoint him with sweet-smelling oil. This discourtesy was a very public rebuke of Christ by a well-known leader.

While Jesus was reclining at the table, the dinner was interrupted by a woman who had a "sin-ful" reputation. (She may have been a prostitute.) She burst into the room and washed the Savior's feet with water, wiping them with her hair, and kissing them. She then anointed Christ's feet with a sweet-smelling perfume that wafted through the dining hall. Simon was incensed that Jesus had allowed this woman, who had lived a publicly sinful life in that town, to touch him.

In this same chapter, Luke tells us that Simon said to himself, "If this man were a prophet, he would know who is touching him and what kind of woman she is—that she is a sinner" (v. 39). Jesus, knowing Simon's private thoughts said, "Simon, I have something to tell you." He went on to state publicly how Simon, by failing to anoint him, had publicly rebuked him. "You did not put oil on my head, but she has poured perfume on my feet. Therefore, I tell you, her many sins have been forgiven—for she loved much. But he who has been forgiven little loves little" (vv. 46-47). The most common act of anointing in Christ's time was the act of welcoming and honoring a guest. It said, *You are very important to me. Everything I have is at your disposal.*

Fear is God's doorbell. It is the way in which we are driven to the arms of our heavenly Father and welcomed into his loving presence. Even after reading and reflecting on all of these meditations, fear still lingers at times. Fears will be with us for as long as we are in this world, for we will always be assaulted by our spiritual enemies. We must learn to "use our fears" in a positive way.

The moment we feel afraid, we are to ring our heavenly Father's doorbell by turning over to him that which causes our fear. Remind yourself that our Father in heaven is not like Simon the Pharisee. Our Father in heaven is so eager to have us trust him in those special moments of fear that he pours out on us the anointing oil of the Holy Spirit who calms our fears with a peace that transcends all human efforts. Jesus said, "Peace I leave with you; my peace I give you. I do not give to you as the world gives. Do not let your hearts be troubled and do not be afraid" (John 14:27). When we come running to the Savior with our deepest fears and surrender them to him, we are anointed with the peace that passes all understanding.

Reflect:
When have you experienced God's anointing peace in the face of fears? Have you ever thought of fear as Jesus' gift, pushing you into his arms? Share your experiences of times of having an amazing, unexpected peace and thereby encourage each other.

DAY 34

You prepare a table before me
in the presence of my
enemies. You anoint my head
with oil; my cup overflows.

—Psalm 23:5

Anointing my head with perfume is one thing, but to have oil poured on my head is …well, not very enticing. I suppose if I lived two thousand years ago, I would feel differently about it, but I just cannot get with it. I have enough problems with the natural oils in my own hair that to have more oil poured on doesn't grab me. Nevertheless, we need to dig into the relevance of the word *oil* today.

Oil is used to heal cuts and bruises. Oil makes things work smoothly. Philip Keller in his book, *A Shepherd Looks at Psalm 23,* tells of the way he used healing oil on his sheep. One of the major problems sheep have is "nose flies": pesky little flies that drive the sheep crazy by crawling up their noses and eventually blocking their breathing and suffocating them. Keller used a homemade mixture of tar, linseed oil, and sulfur, which he spread on the noses of the sheep. Keller writes, "Once the oil had been applied to the sheep's head, there was an immediate change in behavior. Gone was the aggravation; gone the frenzy; gone the irritability and the restlessness. Instead, the sheep would start to feed quietly again, then soon lie down in peaceful contentment" (p. 116).

Oil is the Biblical symbol for the functions of the Holy Spirit. Let's look at three of them. First, one of the devil's best tools is "friction." Isn't it amazing how little wrongs done to us can dominate both our mind and our emotions? You can have a "full cup," and yet one little wrong, hidden in the back of your mind, can cause the dark, quiet drizzle of depression to fall. Think of the flies. Spiritual oppressions can be like flies, constantly irritating and creating far more fear within us than we realize.

We each have our own unique "hot buttons"— mine is a running argument with phone companies. It is utterly amazing to me how, in the best of moments, receiving the wrong bill from the phone company, one that includes a list of cryptic charges that even their CEO's cannot explain, becomes my hot button. What is your friction point or "hot button"?

The Holy Spirit is within us, and if we stop, think, turn, and ask him to bring balance to our lives, he will. He is like the solution Keller talks about that scares the flies away, but with one exception. I do not think the Spirit has an unpleasant aroma. But then, on second thought, he is the fragrance of defeat to the demonic world (see 2 Cor. 2:14).

Keller also mentions the practice of head-butting among the huge male sheep during rutting season. Anointing their heads with oil makes them slippery, so that the butting does not cause too much damage to the animals. One of the best answers to people asking why they should join a specific church is, "It's the best place I know to suffer for Jesus." Churches are not what we expect them to be. While they are harbors of love in life's storms, they can often also be the center of spiritual storms when political power struggles take place; people can be deeply, emotionally scarred by the insensitivities of their spiritual family members. In those head-butting moments, the Holy Spirit will fill our spirits with such an abundance of gratitude and love that we will be enabled to forgive and love one another, preventing damaged or broken relationships from happening.

A second function of the Spirit is to fill us with the oil of gladness. Isaiah writes, "Provide for those who grieve in Zion—to bestow on them a crown of beauty instead of ashes, the oil of gladness instead of mourning, and a garment of praise instead of a spirit of despair" (61:3). If we allow the Spirit to flood us, an inner joy will radiate out through our deeds of listening love.

Oil can also be a symbol of light, as it was the fuel for lamps to bring light to banish the darkness. Jesus said that he was the light of the world and then went on to say that we, too, are to be the light of the world. Christ's Spirit dwells in us, and we become the lamp through which his light shines into this world. The Scriptures are filled with pictures of golden lampstands burning the oil of the Spirit. The lampstand represents the spiritual body of Christ, and the oil burning and casting light represents the Spirit dwelling in it.

Another function of the oil of the Spirit is to provide us with the knowledge that we have been chosen to carry out the calling God has given us. Usually our feelings of insignificance and insecurity are caused by a lack of concern for others. One of the greatest spiritual prisons is self-concern. Those who have learned the joy of sacrifice for others have also experienced a continuing freedom from the fear of insignificance. As the Spirit of God flows from us in torrents of living water (John 7:38), freedom from the fear of failure and feelings of insignificance are washed away. The Spirit enables us to do the good works God has planned for us from all eternity (Eph. 2:10). The Holy Spirit assures us that we have been specifically chosen by God, and that he has his plans to prosper and bless us in his service (Jer. 29:11).

Reflect:

In what ways has, and does, the "oil" of the Holy Spirit quiet your spirit in those restless and insecure moments? How has God's Spirit eased the frictions inflicted by others?

DAY 35

You prepare a table before me
in the presence of my
enemies. You anoint my
head with oil; **my cup
overflows.**

—Psalm 23:5

Whether half empty or half full, our consumerism cups are certainly never full; some of our culture's favorite mantras are "shop until you drop," and "the one with the most toys wins." The Mall of America is for many the Mecca of capitalism.

The world's method of operation has a long tradition: keep changing styles—keep up the demand for new goods. Above all, don't let anyone think his cup is full. Make people live in the fear that they don't have enough, or that they don't have enough of the *right stuff*. Then when they finally feel that they do have enough, keep them fearful that they might lose what they have. Perhaps this strategy works so well, because people actually will lose what they have. The reason so many people's consumerism cups are never filled is because of the God-shaped hole in their souls. Without the proper remedy, being filled by him, all joy from other substitutes will sooner or later drain away.

Have you ever realized how contrary the spirit of this age is to "my cup overflows"? Think about these words: "How great is the love the Father has lavished on us, that we should be called children of God! And that is what we are!" (1 John 3:1). I love the word *lavished*. God's love is poured out so that it flows out of the cup, runs all over the table, and down onto the floor. The greatest treasure in the universe, the love of God, is given so freely that the only verb that describes it is "lavished." The hymn writer stated it well: "Could we with ink the ocean fill, and were the skies of parchment made, were every stalk on earth a quill, and every man a scribe by trade. To write the love of God above, would drain the ocean dry, nor could the scroll contain the whole, though stretched from sky to sky" (*The Love of God*, Frederick M. Lehman, 1917).

Reflect:
Make a list of the ways God has blessed you. Can you see how your cup is overflowing?

WRAP-UP

Conclude this section by writing a meditation. You will notice that the next two pages are designed to hold the thoughts you write. (I hope you will need much more space—these blank pages are only starters.)

List the ways in which your cup is full with temporal blessings on the first page. Then list all the spiritual blessings that fill your cup on the second page. Remember, God has blessed you so much that your cup is overflowing. How and where is it spilling out God's goodness onto others?

WRITE YOUR RESPONSE

WRITE YOUR RESPONSE

Security

Surely goodness and love
[mercy] will follow
me all the days of my life,
and I will dwell in the house
of the Lord forever.

—Psalm 23:6

Verse 6 ends with security in this life and forever. We will dwell in God's house forever, after a life filled with goodness and mercy. Here are the real, eternal reasons for celebration. They are the blessings of eternal life, which we can begin to enjoy right now!

DAY 36

Surely goodness and love
[mercy] will follow
me all the days of my life,
and I will dwell in the house
of the Lord forever.

—Psalm 23:6

The modern church must remember the story of Graham Staines, a missionary serving in Orrissa. Married with, two sons and a daughter, Graham faithfully served his Savior for over twenty years in an area of several counties (districts), quietly ministering to the needs of the poor. One night, around midnight, he and his two sons decided they could travel no further that night on their journey home, so they settled down to sleep in their jeep.

Hindu terrorists, concerned about a massive turning to Christ by the *dalits* (outcasts) in the area, were on a rampage, persecuting Christians to try to stem this tide of people turning to Christ. They found Graham and his two sons sleeping in their jeep. Quietly, they poured gasoline on the vehicle and pressed long poles against the doors of the car so that the Staines could not escape. Then they lit the gas and burned up the car and its passengers.

News of this atrocity spread rapidly throughout the nation. "India Today," India's equivalent of "Time Magazine," pictured India hanging on a cross on its cover. India mourned the death of this sacrificial servant of the poor. The funeral of Graham and his two sons was shown on national TV. At their funeral Gloria Staines, Graham's widow, and her daughter sang these words for India to hear: "Because he lives, I can face tomorrow, because he lives, all fear is gone." What must the non-Christian Indians have thought, as they listened to that line, "All fear is gone"?

How could a widow and her daughter sing that all fear is gone when her husband and two sons had been so brutally, mercilessly burned to death? Where was her longing for revenge? How could she say, "All fear is gone"? What was the source of her courageous love?

Mrs. Staines could sing these words, because she knew the meaning of the little word "surely," just as David knew it. The solid rock, upon which her life and those of her family was built was the truth that Jesus Christ was risen, and in him, they had eternal life. Not only could they forgive, they could also find freedom from fear from the peace of knowing that Jesus saves.

It is the last section and the last verse of Psalm 23. David wraps up this beautiful Psalm in a glorious, mountain-top statement that begins with the word *surely*. Freedom from fear flows from all who can say, "Surely"—certainly—absolutely. It means I am confident, I know, I am positive. Some metaphors to express this same, strong confidence in the power and protection of this God David so trusts are: a rock, a solid foundation, a refuge, a fortress. "To you I call, O LORD my Rock" (Psalm 28:1).

Calling God his Rock is David's way of saying that God surely can be trusted. His Word is absolute. It cannot be doubted. God can be trusted in all situations to be a "rock" of defense, a solid fortress, a refuge in times of trouble. When we trust God as our rock, we attain freedom from fear. Fear fills us in direct proportion to our lack of trust. It all begins and ends with trust. The more we trust God, the more we will be free from fear. Fear pours in when we doubt God and instead rely upon ourselves. Trust and obey, and fear flies away.

When God created us, he made us in his image and in his likeness. Among other things, this means that he created us with the ability to trust him, and in that trust, to build a relationship and a bond of deep and lasting love. He demonstrated his love for Adam and Eve by giving them every imaginable thing in a garden called Eden. In the middle of that garden he placed the highest gift of all, the gift of the opportunity to trust him by obeying him. He placed the tree of the knowledge of good and evil in the middle of the garden and commanded them not to eat its fruit or they would die. In doing this, he gave them an opportunity to trust him—to have an ongoing love relationship with the Creator forever. It was for this reason that God created humans in his likeness. As long as our two parents trusted God, they would live in freedom from fear.

Adam and Eve failed, and instead of trusting God's Word, they followed their own selfish desires:

> When the woman saw that the fruit of the tree was good for food and pleasing to the eye, and also desirable for gaining wisdom, she took some and ate it. She also gave some to her husband, who was with her, and he ate it. Then the eyes of both of them were opened, and they realized they were naked; so they sewed fig leaves together and made coverings for themselves (Gen. 3:6-7).

Fear began when Adam and Eve failed to trust God. Relationships are built on trust. Trusting is the other side of the coin of love. Love and trust must go together. Without trust, love cannot exist. Love is trusting, and trusting is love. By their lack of trust in God's Word, they destroyed the love that existed between them and God, thereby entering into a world of fear.

God has given us all another opportunity to trust him, and in that trust to express our love for him. When we do, our relationship with God is restored so that we can enjoy freedom from fear: "For God so loved the world that he gave his one and only Son, that whoever believes in him shall not perish but have eternal life" (John 3:16). This beautiful, well-known verse of Scripture is the "surely," the New Testament certainty about God, which, when trusted, brings us freedom from fear.

Reflect:

Our greatest challenge in life is to trust God as a little child trusts his or her parents. We demand understanding, but Jesus tells us that only by being like little children can we enter the kingdom of heaven (Matt. 18:3). Ask God for the gift of a simple, child-like trust. Practice it, and find freedom from fear today. Say "surely" many times throughout your day as you think of God's care for you. Let there be "no doubt about it!"

DAY 37

Surely **goodness** and love
[mercy] will follow
me all the days of my life,
and I will dwell in the house
of the Lord forever.

—Psalm 23:6

Two things will "pursue" us throughout our lifetime if we trust God: goodness and mercy. Mercy is also translated as love or loving kindness. First, we will look at the word *goodness;* in the next reading we will consider mercy, or loving kindness. Goodness deals with God's treatment of all the things that happen to us—our circumstances. Mercy or love deals with that which goes wrong inside of us and God's handling of that.

Jacob was born in India with twisted legs—he could never walk. He wore thongs on his hands and "bumped" himself along by swinging his body forward. By trusting Christ, Jacob lived in freedom from fear and in heavenly joy. He was an example of God's goodness in taking tragedy and turning it out for good.

Jacob had a special way with children. He explained that they didn't have to look up to him. Since his legs were twisted and he could not use them, he was permanently on a child's level. They could look him in the eye. And in child-like ways they accepted him, for he loved them dearly and they responded to that love, rather than to his strange condition.

Jacob organized a number of Children's Clubs, and many children attended them regularly. One day someone told Jacob about Mission India's Children's Bible Clubs and the wonderful curriculum that they offered. Jacob decided to try to get some of these courses for his children's clubs, even though the office was 250 kilometers away.

He pushed himself along, using his thong-covered hands as feet and swinging his body forward step-by-step. He boarded the necessary buses and finally made his way to the Mission India office some 250 kilometers from his home. The office staff were surprised to see him. They were amazed at the man's determination to get the Bible courses for his children. They wondered how he could travel all that distance by swinging his torso, "standing" on his hands. The thongs on his hands were worn down almost to nothing by the time he arrived. Many pictures were taken as he told the story of how he had turned his handicap into an advantage for reaching children for Christ. Children's Bible Club materials were assembled for his children and sent on ahead as he made his way over the 250 kilometers back to his home.

Jacob's story is a demonstration of God's goodness. God does one of two things for us. He will either protect us from evil by not allowing it to happen, or if it does come into our lives, he will turn it to good for those who trust him. Jacob's case is one of the most startling examples of the latter that I've ever heard. He radiates joy in spite of having to crawl along on his hands. His grotesquely twisted legs are a picture of the brokenness in this world, but the smile on his face and the life transformation coming to the hundreds of boys and girls in his club from God's love flowing from him is a testimony to God's goodness and his power.

There are many things in life that make us wonder about God's goodness. How can a good God permit all of the evil in this world to happen? The answer is found in the way God created us. He did not create us to be robots, but instead he created us with a will, in his image, to be able to choose either to live in love with him or to reject his offer of love. Love is real only if it is not forced.

Let's imagine that you have a daughter who is extremely rebellious and causes you great heartache. It is not hard to picture that, but imagine that you became so weary of the constant discouragement and pain that you brought her to a hospital and had her brain wired so that you could control her behavior. What reaction did you have right now? Such a thought is abhorrent, because it would destroy your daughter. Huxley's "Brave New World" is a picture of destroyed humanity when it is programmed, not by wires, but by "happiness drugs." We would no longer be human and capable of choosing true love if we were wired or drugged to control our actions and choices.

Paul states it this way: "No, in all these things we are more than conquerors through him who loved us" (Rom. 8:37). Remember his words to Job in the midst of Job's suffering. "Where were you when I laid the earth's foundation? Tell me if you understand" (Job 38:4). We are humans, and God's *goodness* preserves that while making us *more than conquerors*.

Reflect:
Which of these illustrations help you the most in driving out fear?

DAY 38

Surely goodness and **love**
[mercy] will follow
me all the days of my life,
and I will dwell in the house
of the Lord forever.

—Psalm 23:6

There is another word here—the word is *love*. It is God's amazing and unmerited love, which pursues us and which flows through us to touch others. God's love falls equally on all of us, just as the sunshine falls equally on all who are sun bathing on a beach. As the sun doesn't discriminate, so God's love shows no discrimination. It embraces the worst, as well as the best among us. Think of a crowded beach without any shade. It doesn't matter to the sun how many people are on the beach; all get the sunshine equally.

It is hard for us to understand that God's love for us is not merited. He does not love us because of the good we do. He loves us because of whom he made us to be: creatures in his image and in his likeness (Gen. 1:26). His goodness provides protection from external enemies, and his love provides protection from the consequences of our sinful natures and consequent failures.

"How great is the love the Father has lavished on us, that we should be called children of God! And that is what we are!" (1 John 3:1). Think of a glass. Someone is filling it. In joyous abandon, he continues to pour, and the full glass spills over, splashing its contents on everything around it. That's a picture of the love of God being lavished on us—it is so much that we cannot contain it.

The main reason we cannot contain the love of God is because of sin. That sin shuts the door to the love of God. Our guilt over what we have done wrong slams our brain shut to considering that anyone could love us, even God himself. But once we understand the love of God and consider the fact that God, through the sacrifice of Jesus Christ, has made it possible for him to love us, we are transformed from the inside out.

The love of God is the single greatest power for banishing fear from our lives. The pictures drawn in the Bible are so awesome in their power. I often return to the powerful picture described in Zephaniah 3:16-17. This verse starts with a strange command. "Don't let your hands hang limp." That is a picture of the "blues," of depression. The devil wants us to walk through life with limp hands as a symbol of our hopeless situation. God counters that picture with a detailed explanation of his transforming love. Here are five ways God loves us:

The Lord your God is with you.

He is mighty to save.

He will take great delight in you.

He will quiet you with his love.

He will rejoice over you with singing.

That last line says it all. Remember the times you have held a little baby and quieted it. Since God has cleansed you totally (through Jesus Christ's sacrifice and your faith and trust in him), he is now spiritually holding you as a little child and rejoicing over you with singing. If that isn't enough reason to banish fear, then what is? God, the Creator of the universe, loves you with infinitely more love than we can even love our own precious little children.

Reflect:

Take the thought of God rejoicing over you so much that he is singing about you, and apply it to your fears. Each time you are troubled, think of your position in the love of Christ as described in this reading.

DAY 39

Surely goodness and love [mercy] **will follow me** all the days of my life, and I will dwell in the house of the Lord forever.

—Psalm 23:6

Francis Thompson's famous poem describes God as the "Hound of Heaven." Some translators render "will follow me" as "he pursues me." Our LORD does pursue us.

I look back over fifty-plus years of ministry, and I am overwhelmed by God's goodness and love. Every time I look back, I see something new. His goodness and mercy have certainly pursued me. I have experienced many physical problems during my lifetime. I've had triple by-pass heart surgery, followed by three heart attacks during my sixties; I have six stents; I've had emergency surgery for a broken gall bladder which was spewing poison over my insides; a year later I had the same kind of surgery for a burst appendix; I've had a small blockage in my left eye which permanently blocks much of the vision in that eye; I've had kidney stone surgery; and I've had diverticulitis. I feel a little like Paul, several times over, reciting all these varied thorns in my flesh; and yet at seventy-five, God's grace has always been sufficient, providing me with the energy and the strength to continue to teach, preach, and write. Surely I have been pursued by his goodness and mercy!

One of my associate pastors told of going home late one night, walking alone through a rather dark area, but being completely oblivious to any lurking danger. Sometime later a young man who had recently decided to follow Jesus came to him and asked if he could join his church. When asked why he wanted to join his church, he told this story. "Do you remember, Pastor, one night a few months ago when you were walking alone, going home through a dangerous neighborhood?" The pastor thought for a moment and said that he did remember the night. The young man continued, "I was following you, intending to rob you. But I was frightened off when you were joined by two men who walked on either side of you, so I disappeared."

My associate responded, "But I was alone that night. I did not have anyone with me." The young man adamantly refused to believe it, and insisted that he had seen two large, muscular men walking with him. The pastor concluded that it must have been two angels sent to guard him at that moment.

Do you believe in guardian angels? "For he will command his angels concerning you to guard you in all your ways." This statement from Psalm 91:11 is also echoed in Isaiah 63:9 and in Daniel 3:28. God *does* send guardian angels. Jesus tells us that angels are assigned to pursue us and to protect us, beginning when we are only children. "See that you do not look down on one of these little ones [children]. For I tell you that their angels in heaven always see the face of my Father in heaven" (Matt. 18:10).

One of our problems is that we do not see things as God does, because we are too small, and we are creatures of time. Little children have temper tantrums when they cannot get their own way. They do not see things from their parents' perspective. A little one wants to go in the water on a windy day when the rip tide is great (a common occurrence on the east side of Lake Michigan), and there is danger that she will be suddenly swept away. Mom notices that her daughter is entering the dangerous current, and she runs through the sand as fast as she can go, catching her little girl just in time. The little girl, however, is not happy about being stopped, and she throws a temper tantrum. She does not understand the danger she was about to face.

We wrestle with God. Why is something that is so bad happening in our life? Why don't you answer me and do what I want, Lord? God's answer is very simple. *Like a parent chasing a child that is constantly near danger, so I am chasing you. I am pursuing you. My goodness, my mercy, and my love will always be running after you every day (and every night) of your life.*

Are you afraid? Are things not working the

way you want them to? Maybe God isn't doing what you want, and you find yourself terrified of the future. Remember, just as a parent chases a child who is in danger to rescue the child, so God pursues all of us with his love and protective care. Don't be afraid. God sees the real danger, even when we cannot, and he is always with us to protect us.

Reflect:

Have you had times when you wanted a solution to some problem and God would not give it, or at least did not give the one you thought you wanted? What was your reaction?

DAY 40

Surely goodness and love
[mercy] will follow
me all the days of
my life,
and I will dwell in the house
of the Lord forever.

— Psalm 23:6

The pastor began his New Year's Eve sermon by saying that it seemed to him that the passing of time was much like a roll of toilet paper. The closer you get to the end, the faster it goes around. Time seems to move slowly for little children and for teens. They are always looking forward to their next birthday, or to graduation, or to marriage. It seems to pass so slowly in our early years, but the older we get, the faster time seems to slip by.

In the last phase of life, summer seems to shorten to only a couple of weeks, spring and fall each seem to last only a week, and only winter feels as if it lingers a bit—but even in lingering, it moves by quickly. Looking back over one's life is like remembering yesterday. It is hard to imagine that a lifetime was once something with an end so distant that we could not imagine it ever coming, and now it seems to be something that is nearing quickly. Where does the time go?

Just what is time? Think of the past, the present, and the future. Do we ever experience the present? Does time stop some days, while we enjoy a picnic? A clock's batteries may wear out, but time does not, and it keeps marching on. In a sense, we never really experience the present. What is "now"? It is gone the moment you read the question. The first time you read the question, that time is already gone. It is history. If you read it for the second time, the first and second readings are already in the past. The present is never captured while we are in time. Time consists only of the past and the future. The moment the past is over, the future is there. To truly experience the present is to make time stop. Time is an eternal "now."

That always frightened me as a boy. An eternal "now" can sound awfully boring. We are people of life, and life is growth. What does heaven mean if we cannot celebrate for eternity all the past wonders of God's love? Paul tells us that there are three eternal things: "faith, hope and love." Both faith and hope imply a future. How can one hope, when there is nothing to which to look forward? When I finally captured the reality that we will still be anticipating things in eternity, and that we will still be hoping, I decided that heaven would not be that bad after all. Peter tells us that we have been born again to a "living hope;" this means that our anticipation of great things will neither ever disappoint, nor ever fade (I Pet. 1:3).

I believe that heaven will be a wonderful present, a "now" made up of both the past and the future. It will be something entirely different than anything we can now imagine. We will be able to look back at God's goodness and love and see how it followed and pursued us all the days of our lives. It will take an eternity to unravel all the marvelous gifts of God and see them in their full beauty.

The famous "river vision" in Ezekiel 47 is the picture of life. Each good work God did through us started with a little trickle of goodness and then expanded far beyond anything we can see in this life. We do not know now all that God has done with us, but we will know then. We will see the goodness and love that flowed from us, something like the wake that follows a speed boat. It starts small and spreads far out behind the boat.

The goodness and mercy that pursues us every day of our lives is God's goodness flowing through us. We will be able to look back, and we will be surprised to see how God multiplied the little good things we did (the deeds we did not even realize we were doing) and how he blessed them and made them into "wakes" of his goodness, following us in ways which we never could have imagined. Heaven will be celebrating God's goodness, not just *to* us, but also flowing *through* us. We are his temple now, and his goodness flows out of us.

God's goodness and love "follow us" like a wake follows a boat, growing wider and wider, just as a small stream flows on to become a mighty river. In heaven we will see the rivers of God's love which flowed from us, to and through others, throughout all the days of our lives.

Reflect:

We can start experiencing a little of heaven now by looking back, not at the bad, but at the good. Find some little rivers of goodness that started from your life, and reflect on them. How did they grow? And as you meditate on these things, watch fear disappear.

DAY 41

Surely goodness and love
[mercy] will follow
me all the days of my life,
and **I will dwell in
the house**
of the Lord forever.

—Psalm 23:6

I illustrated the cover of the *The New You*, a book about Christ living in us, with a picture of a beautiful house at twilight, welcoming us to enter as the inviting, warm light streamed from its windows. It is a book about the way in which we build our self-image. In the book, I compare Mt. Vernon, George Washington's home, to the White House, asking which one terrorists would choose to attack. Obviously they would be far more interested in attacking the White House, because it is occupied by one of the most important persons in the world, the

President of the United States. Mt. Vernon is an unoccupied museum. God created us in his image, as the mansion in which he dwells through his Holy Spirit. We ought to derive our importance and build our self-image on the basis of the one who lives in us!

Christ dwells in us: "I have been crucified with Christ and I no longer live, but Christ lives in me. The life I live in the body, I live by faith in the Son of God, who loved me and gave himself for me" (Gal 2:20). The warmth of his light, his Spirit, streams out of us, just like the warm glow of the light streaming from the windows of a country house at twilight.

David pictures heaven as a house. He seems to have left the imagery of a shepherd behind as he describes eternity as being the LORD's house, his dwelling place for all eternity. Think about the word *house,* and what this tells us. We will not be homeless after we die, if we are followers of Jesus and believe in him. We will be in our Father's house forever. Hell is eternal homelessness. It is being alone and separated from God in eternity.

The word *house* brings to mind many things. It suggests security, belonging, having a family, and a place to be. Heaven is a house—a warm, secure place for a giant family. One of our daughters just bought a new little house. She has been renting until now, but now she owns her own home. She is delighted to settle down, put down roots, and have a place to call hers. Her family can gather with her in her little house. She can make it beautiful and inviting. And she is excited about doing so.

All of those emotions are connected with spending an eternity in the house of the LORD. When we pass from this period of life to the final and eternal period, we will enter a secure house. We will never be homeless in eternity. We will have a family and an unimaginable house, because it will be the house of the LORD. Many of us think of heaven as some place "up there." However, Revelation 21:1-3 tells us, that the house of the LORD will be down here:

> Then I saw a new heaven and a new earth, for the first heaven and the first earth had passed away, and there was

no longer any sea. I saw the Holy City, the New Jerusalem, coming down out of heaven from God, prepared as a bride beautifully dressed for her husband. And I heard a loud voice from the throne saying, "Now the dwelling of God is with men, and he will live with them. They will be his people, and God himself will be with them and be their God."

God will create a new earth, and on this earth he will gather his people together in a new way that David describes as living in the "LORD'S House." It will be a place of perfect harmony. Everything will be put back together again. Jesus will dwell there, and his glory and light will illuminate it, and there will be no more night. It is in that eternal daylight that we will be able to have perfect hindsight and foresight and never leave the present. Together, we will rejoice over all the little trickles of goodness that flowed from our lives without our noticing and which God made into mighty Mississippi Rivers of blessings to others. We will anticipate with joy the great discoveries we will make about God's infinite love, wisdom, and power; and we will never be disappointed, for we will have a "living hope" in heaven (1 Peter 1:3).

We will be in the "LORD's house," experiencing all the wonderful emotions connected with having the loving home that we can now only dream of. We will have a place forever. There will be no fear of losing it, no fear of change, and no fear of moving. Our dwelling will be everything and more that we can dream of as we rehearse the past and anticipate the new discoveries of the future.

Reflect:

Have you been able to experience conquered fear? What has happened to the fears of your past failures? What has happened to your fears of the future?

DAY 42

Surely goodness and love
[mercy] will follow
me all the days of my life,
and I will dwell in the house
of the Lord **forever.**

—Psalm 23:6

What is eternity? I've never experienced the future, have you? I am always looking forward to it, but when it comes, it is instantly gone, and it becomes a memory. What is it like to be outside of time and yet be looking forward and also looking back? What does the word "forever" mean?

Heaven without memory denies reflection on the marvelous love of God. We must be able to see where we have come from. We must have a new comprehension of the awesome love of God, demonstrated not only by his rescue of us, but also by his use of us to reflect his love to others.

However, in heaven we will not be merely looking back. In heaven we will also be looking forward. It will not be a stagnant place. It is eternal *life*, and life is not stagnant. It is growth. We grow or we die. In heaven, we will grow, not only by looking back, but also by being in an eternal present of looking forward and exploring ever-expanding vistas of the beauty and awesome wonder of a God without limits.

Now we look back and are filled with guilt over all the wrong we have done. We look forward and cannot see what is there, and our guilt makes us afraid. That is the world in which we live now.

Somehow, in some mysterious way, there will be an eternal present that embraces the past with wonder at how God multiplied everything good that we did in his name, and there will be a future in which we see his infinite love and beauty constantly unfolding. No, we cannot fully understand everything now, but we will then. *And all fear will be gone.*

We cannot yet understand being in all three dimensions at one time: the past, the present, and the future. But that is what constitutes eternity. Paul wrote: "And now these three remain: faith, hope and love. But the greatest of these is love" (1 Cor.13:13). Love is not the only eternal virtue in heaven, but it is the greatest. Even so, we will also all have perfect faith. We will trust God and each other, never doubting either. Talk about freedom from fear! Trust is the cement that holds us together. Heaven on this new earth will be a place where everything has been put back together in perfect harmony! We will know a perfect, all-encompassing unity! But in addition to living in perfect trust forever, we will be anticipating, looking forward, with what Peter calls a "living hope" (1 Peter 1:3).

What is a "living hope?" Dad was a chemist and, as such, he was always anticipating new discoveries in his research. He told me that the discoveries were always very exciting at the moment he first found something new, but the excitement soon fell away. He defined "living hope" as discovering new wonders about God and never having the excitement of knowing God more and more fully diminish or grow old. Every new discovery that we will make about God in eternity will have an eternal excitement. That is "living" hope. That is savoring each new discovery with the same joyous level of excitement for all of eternity.

Look at all the beauty of nature. Think of the colors of fall, the flowers of spring, the snow of winter, and the sparkling lakes of summer. All of this will be heaven, for heaven will be here on earth.

What better way to conclude this devotion than with John's beautifully inspired description of heaven:

> Then I saw a new heaven and a new earth, for the first heaven and the first earth had passed away, and there was no longer any sea. I saw the Holy City, the New Jerusalem, coming down out of heaven from God, prepared as a bride beautifully dressed for her husband. And I heard a loud voice from the throne saying, "Now the dwelling of God is with men, and he will live with

them. They will be his people, and God himself will be with them and be their God. He will wipe every tear from their eyes. There will be no more death or mourning or crying or pain, for the old order of things has passed away (Rev. 21:1-4).

Reflect:

Does this vision of eternity, combined with understanding God's goodness and love, dispel your fears?

WRAP-UP

With your family or group, review the seven key words and phrases:

1. *Surely*: What experiences did you have with freedom from fear as you meditated on the concept of certainly—"surely"?

2. *Goodness*: How did the concept of *"goodness"* affect you?

3. *Love*: What refreshing thoughts came to mind as you reflected on God's unconditional love for you?

4. *Will follow me…*: You've walked through some dark valleys. What goodness and love did you find in them?

5. *All the days of my life…*: Have you thought of how God's goodness and love are flowing from you to others every day of your life? Have you seen just a little of God's multiplying power, expanding the goodness that originated with something you did?

6. *I will dwell in the house…*: What warm, good thoughts does the word "house" bring to mind?

7. *Forever…*: Are you frightened by "forever"? If you are, did this last meditation help relieve your fears?

Reaching America
County by County

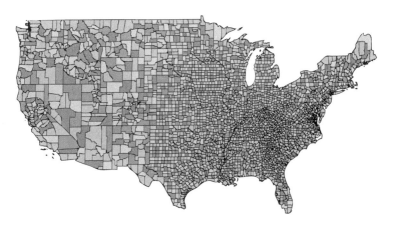

Share with your neighbor's why
you are not afraid.

Mail a copy of *Freedom From Fear* to everyone
in your county. For more information contact us
at reachingamerica@projectphilipministries.org.

Why Give?

40 days of simple and easy to read meditations exploring five profound reasons why joy flows foremost out of giving.

(Available in both print and e-book formats)

58RVillisedr

Why Pray?

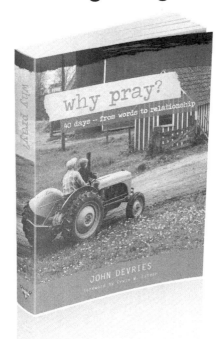

40 easy to read meditations about the joy of communicating to our Heavenly Father and trusting in Him.

(Available in both print and e-book formats)

Marryline
Cit6 6222.20

Coming soon
Who Do You Look Like?

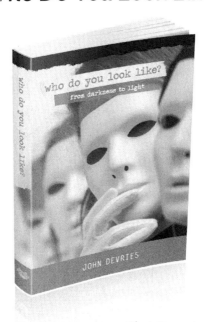

Meditations which encourage Christians to value
themselves as God's image bearers, temples of the
Lord Jesus, and as co-heirs with Christ. This book
will help believers know how to reign with Christ.
(Available in both print and e-book formats)